VICTORIAN NEEDLEPOINT

VICTORIAN NEEDLEPOINT

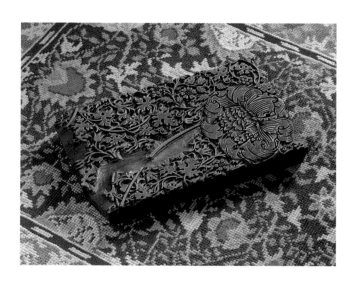

BETH RUSSELL

Special photography by John Greenwood

CRESCENT BOOKS
New York

For Peter, Nick and Paul

First published in Great Britain in 1989
by Anaya Publishers Ltd, 49 Neal Street, London WC2H 9PJ

This 1990 edition published by Crescent Books
Distributed by Crown Publishers, Inc., 225 Park Avenue South,
New York, New York 10003

The Publishers would like to thank the following:
The London Graphic Centre, Long Acre, London WC2 for the loan of
the easel and brushes
The Thimble Society, Grey's Antique Market, London W1 for the loan
of antique needlework tools
Editor: Judy Walker
Charts: Jil Shipley, John Hutchinson, Richard Phipps
Designer: Sheila Volpe
Special photography: John Greenwood

ISBN 0-517-02780-1
hgfedcba

Typeset by Tradespools, Frome, Somerset
Colour origination by Marfil, S. L. (Madrid)
Printed in Spain by Edime, S. A. (Madrid)
D. L. M-1.065-1990

CONTENTS

INTRODUCTION

My need to be creative has come, I think, from my family background. Three-quarters of the furniture in our house in Llansamlet, in South Wales, was made by my father. With the minimum of tools and space, he produced truly beautiful chairs, cabinets, beds and even wardrobes. I became accustomed to seeing him dovetailing joints, carving claw and ball feet, and French polishing. A great deal of this was done at home, and I was allowed to help with the sandpapering and polishing. There seemed nothing that my father could not teach himself to do: he painted in oils and watercolours, tried beadwork, etched glass, made shoes, sewed and cooked – and all well.

Much of our linen had been embroidered by my mother's sister and all the curtains and covers were made at home. We slept on feather mattresses (the feathers from my mother's family farm), between crisply starched sheets, and there were carved swans' heads at the foot of my bed. Even my dolls had their own expanding table and carved chairs.

I was brought up to believe that the best things were those you made yourself. Bought objects were viewed most critically. Later on, my husband was a little startled when I suggested that whatever we needed we could make ourselves!

My introduction to the style of decorative art which has remained my favourite took place on my seventh birthday. As a treat, I was allowed, on my own, to listen to a musical rehearsal in the Brangwyn Hall in Swansea. Magnificent panels, painted by Sir Frank Brangwyn (1867–1956) originally for the House of Lords, cover every wall (see the endpapers). The immensely strong shapes and rich colours are awe-inspiring; there is not an inch of plain background. People, fruit and animals peep out from, or merge into, the dense, curving foliage. I do not think there is a straight line in one of the panels. It is this first deep impression of lines that sweep and move, and the generosity of design, that has stayed with me.

Frank Brangwyn had worked with William Morris's company. His trips to the East helped to develop his highly personal style, but the strong drawings, rich colours and romantic conception were shared by Morris and many of his contemporaries.

Much later, I continued to be drawn towards the work of this particular group of artists. When I married, *Bachelor's Button* was the first Morris fabric we chose to cover chairs and to make a large round tablecloth. Our second son was born into a room decorated with Morris's dramatic black and white *Indian* wallpaper and we had *Marigold* in the drawing room.

The years when the children were small were filled with curtain and clothes making. I joined a pottery class as we needed jugs and fruit dishes. Photography was an important hobby. We also developed an interest in children's illustrated books and began collecting Kate Greenaway, Arthur Rackham, Edmund Dulac and Walter Crane. My favourite book is *The Ancient*

Left: Swans' heads at the foot of my bed, carved by my father when I was a child. Teddy's sweater was my first attempt at knitting. *Right:* One of the doll's chairs made for me by my father, photographed here in Kelmscott Manor, William Morris's home in Gloucestershire from 1871 until his death in 1896. The needlepoint chair seat is a miniature version of *Lodden* (page 30). For details of how to adapt any of the designs in the book, see page 105.

Mariner, illustrated by Willy Pogany. These artists belong to the same period as Brangwyn and Morris – the seeds sown so long before were beginning to sprout.

I started work at the Royal School of Needlework in London one autumn. At 25 Princes Gate, in what must be one of the loveliest buildings in London, I was surrounded by beautiful carving and mouldings, original Walter Crane paintings, hand-blocked wallpaper (also said to be by Crane) and a plethora of designs from the late 1800s and early 1900s. I became familiar with Appleton's yarn colours – there are over 400 and the ability to readily distinguish between them is a slowly learned art. Now I find that I think of colours only in terms of their Appleton names and numbers, even when buying clothes.

The very formal atmosphere when I started at the Royal School of Needlework was reminiscent of my days at college. Several people did not speak to me for weeks because (I later learned) I occasionally wore trousers. However, my memories are of a sun-drenched room with high ceilings, tall French windows leading on to a terrace and a huge garden with a Japanese-looking tree in the centre. This delightful room was the shop, which some years later I was asked to run.

Given free rein in the shop, I bought threads and embroidery tools I had not previously known existed. I searched for interesting books to sell, and the shop became known as a treasure trove for embroiderers. Customers were pleased, money started coming in, and I was thrilled. Old designs were rediscovered and new ones created. The *Daily Telegraph* frequently told its readers about us. It was a very exciting period in my life.

However, success brought its own problems. As we expanded and began selling to other shops and outlets overseas, the business side became more complex. I was promoted to sales manager and, to allow more time for administration and to accommodate more people in the shop, I moved away from the public (and the sun) into the basement. I felt that the challenge and the fun had gone. After twelve years, I left. Sadly, 25 Princes Gate has since been sold and the shop is no more.

Eager to start afresh and do my own designing, I happened to learn that Sanderson's (who own the original printing blocks) were re-launching some of their range of William Morris's wallpapers. I realized that *Trellis* and *Celandine* would both translate beautifully into needlepoint, and *Trellis* became my first adaptation for needlepoint.

I had already tried most forms of embroidery. I had also done a great deal of dressmaking and knitting, always to my own designs. I liked playing with colour and styles while sorting out the mathematical problems of rows and stitches. At the Royal School, I had been exposed to their fabulous collection of all types of embroidery, but I recognized I lacked the skill and patience required for many of them, such as goldwork and lace. I prefer making things that have a definite purpose.

Selina Winter at the Royal School introduced me to the technique of needlepoint, or canvaswork, and I completed a stitch sampler for a bedroom stool. Through this and the daily experience of helping customers with their choice of colours and designs to go in their homes, I became intrigued with the challenge of turning rigid squares of canvas into flowing designs with apparently perfect curves. In this, needlepoint is not unlike knitting, and they are also similar in having a practical use. Then there are the colours; how they are used can alter the shape of a leaf, turning it over, making it curl or leaving it quite flat.

Above: The original pear wood block used to print William Morris's *Kennet* fabric. *Top right:* My first solo adventure was to publish *Church Hassocks*. Jean Wells has adapted the designs from *Strawberry Thief* and *Wild Flowers* for Kelmscott church, where Morris is buried.

Every time I solved a problem, I learnt something. Now this aspect of designing gives me the greatest pleasure. The most logical approach to the lovely Morris designs would have been to use them for the surface embroidery or weaving for which they were originally intended, but there is a perverse pleasure in defeating the rigidity of the canvas while retaining as much of the design as possible.

Some designs have proved much easier than others. Sometimes I draw the design directly on the canvas, sometimes on graph paper, so some start life as a painted canvas and others as a charted design.

I always have to decide at the outset the finished size of the article and, according to the intricacy of the design, how coarse a canvas I can afford to have while still permitting enough stitches to retain the detail. Sometimes, especially in the case of rugs which are stitched on coarse canvas, I have to leave out some details. The curves have to look as if they curve, in spite of the 'steps' taken by the stitches.

With tent stitch, there is a special problem: where the stitch is diagonal, and is used for symmetrical curves, the stitches will lie better on one side than on the other. Fortunately, our eyes adjust and often 'see' what we want them to see, making a true symmetry where none exists.

Colours are just as important. I always have a framed-up piece of canvas to hand and use it like a sketch pad. The shades of wool must be stitched to get their true effect. Two colours held in your hand may seem perfect but could be indistinguishable when stitched. In general, colours in wool stitch darker than they look.

My first few designs I did entirely alone, but I am now lucky enough to have found Phyllis Steed, who draws beautifully and can produce immaculate line drawings from my wobbly sketches. I am also lucky to have found some excellent embroiderers, whose stitching is a joy to behold and who can translate my ideas to canvas freehand. Soon, perhaps, my canvas sketch pad will be superfluous, but it would be sad to lose it. I want to stay at the creative end of the action.

Canvas stitching is less taxing than surface embroidery and much harder-wearing. There is a repetitive peacefulness about needlepoint which makes it addictive. If the colours and shapes are good, you will have something lovely to look at, and also to use at the finish.

William Morris expressed this a hundred years ago:

If you want a golden rule that will fit everybody, this is it: Have nothing in your houses that you do not know to be useful, or believe to be beautiful.

THE ARTS AND CRAFTS MOVEMENT

The Arts and Crafts Movement, from which most of my designs are taken, started as a gentle rebellion by a group of artists, designers and architects concerned by the poor standard of design they saw around them in the buildings and furnishings of Victorian England.

After the Industrial Revolution, Britain led the world as the most advanced industrial nation. The advantages of mechanization and mass production were, however, accompanied by the sacrifice of beauty and individuality and the loss of fulfilment for the maker. Speaking to a meeting of industrialists in 1880, William Morris (1834–1896), one of the most influential leaders of the Arts and Crafts Movement, voiced the problem:

> (I) call on you to face the latest danger which civilization is threatened with, a danger of her own breeding: that men in struggling towards the complete attainment of all the luxuries of life for the strongest portion of their race should deprive the whole race of the beauty of life. . . .

Together with the author John Ruskin and the architect A. W. N. Pugin, Morris advocated instead a return to the values of craftsmanship he saw and loved in the designs of the Middle Ages – 'that commoner work, in which all men once shared'.

William Morris was born into a comfortably wealthy family; throughout his life his own money had to help support his work. As a young man at Oxford University, he met Edward Burne-Jones and Dante Gabriel Rossetti, Pre-Raphaelite painters who were to remain his friends for the rest of his life. After university, Morris started training in the offices of the architect Philip Webb, but he was soon invited by Rossetti to join a scheme for decorating the interior of the Oxford Union Library. He quickly recognized his true talents as a designer; in Oxford also he met his wife, Janey, the dark, brooding model for Rossetti's most famous paintings.

Morris adored his wife but the marriage was an unhappy one; she turned away from him to Rossetti, and at their later home, Kelmscott Manor, they lived in a strange *ménage à trois*.

Their first married home (1860–65) was the Red House in Bexleyheath, Kent, a new building commissioned from Philip Webb. The red-brick exterior, considered daring at the time, was completed in just over a year, but I suspect the furnishings took rather longer. Morris insisted on hand-made furniture and hand-finished interiors, and Philip Webb, Rossetti and Burne-Jones were all involved. I like to think of the weekend parties at the Red House with Morris's friends, painting the walls and stencilling the ceilings.

It was Morris's inability to find what he wanted ready-made for his home that caused him to set up his own company, Morris, Marshall, Faulkner & Co. ('the Firm'), in London in 1861. The enormous influence he exercised over design from the 1860s was mostly through the Firm. Wallpapers, furniture, stained glass, and later fabrics and then weaving were all produced under his guidance and often to his design. Morris's designs use clear bright colours, in contrast to the garish tones of the Berlin woolwork embroidery which was then in fashion.

He also worked closely with other leading Victorian designers, among them William De Morgan (1839–1917), whose Persian-coloured ceramic tiles depict fabulous beasts, sailing ships and exotic floral and bird designs. The rich glazes of the tiles are very difficult to capture in needlepoint, but I had to try.

I think of William Morris first and foremost as a pattern designer, and because he rediscovered the forgotten technique of indigo dyeing. But Morris was also a poet; he wrote several novels (the most famous is *News from Nowhere*); he even learnt Icelandic so that he could set about the task of translating the sagas. As if all this were not enough, he was also a brilliant and influential typographer, printing masterpieces such as the *Kelmscott Chaucer* at his own Kelmscott Press in the coach-house of his London home, Kelmscott House, in Hammersmith.

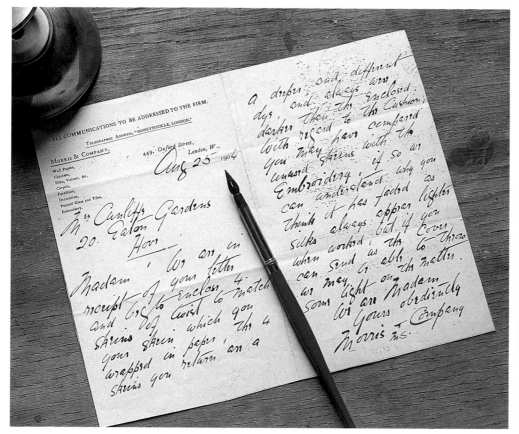

Left: An original letter from Morris & Co., dated 1904, answering a customer's enquiry. It was kindly sent to me by a customer of mine in America.

Below: William Morris in his fifties. This pen and ink drawing is now in Kelmscott Manor.

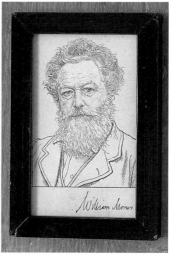

Towards the end of his life, Morris became more and more involved in socialism, spending much of his time writing pamphlets and speaking at public meetings. It was the inevitable result of his search for beauty for all. 'What right have you', he lectured his well-fed audience of industrialists, 'to shut yourself up with beautiful form and colour when you make it impossible for other people to have any share in these things?' The failure of the Firm's ideals was that the hand-made furnishings they produced could only be afforded by the rich.

Yet, when I think of William Morris, however much he may have felt unhappy with the time in which he lived, he must have been pleased with his achievements.

The Arts and Crafts Movement slowly became worldwide and later developed into the style now recognized as Art Nouveau. The name comes from a gallery, L'Art Nouveau, opened in Paris in 1895 by Samuel Bing and decorated by Frank Brangwyn. It displayed work by L. C. Tiffany, Henry van de Velde, Walter Crane, Aubrey Beardsley and many more. The Chicago World's Fair in 1893 exhibited designs by Tiffany & Co., and in the same year Frank Lloyd Wright set up his architectural practice in America. Back in England, the new *Studio* magazine illustrated the work of a rich variety of artists and designers,

including C. F. A. Voysey and Frank Brangwyn.

In *News from Nowhere*, published in 1891, William Morris describes an ideal future society after an imaginary civil war in 1952. The central character in the story falls asleep in Victorian England and wakes in a world where handicrafts and machinery are in harmony. Someone he meets explains the new system:

> The wares which we make are made because they are needed; men make for their neighbours' use as if they are making for themselves, not for a vague market of which they know nothing, and over which they have no control. . . as we are not driven to make a vast quantity of useless things, we have time and resources enough to consider our pleasure in making them. All work which would be irksome to do by hand is done by immensely improved machinery; and in all work which it is a pleasure to do by hand, machinery is done without.

Happily, there is no machine for needlepoint so we can take as great a pleasure in it as we choose. I hope you will derive as much enjoyment from developing these designs as I have in finding them for you.

STRAWBERRY THIEF

Above: Strawberry Thief
furnishing fabric is still available
today from Liberty's of London.

Right: My three *Strawberry Thief*
designs were made up as chair
seats and a cushion by Jean Wells
at Kelmscott Manor. They look
at home in the Old Hall, in front
of the prettily faded original
Strawberry Thief fabric designed
by William Morris in the 1880s.
The portrait of Jane Morris is by
Rossetti.

This popular textile design by William Morris
was printed at Merton Abbey in Surrey about
1883. Morris hated the lurid colours produced by the
new aniline dyes. He wanted to recreate the colours of
the historical textiles he loved, so he went to great
trouble to research the techniques of vegetable dyeing. The indigo discharge method by which *Strawberry Thief* was produced was lengthy and complex,
and I think Morris must have been extremely pleased
with its success.

Sometimes a single Morris pattern can inspire a
whole series of designs. In this case, different elements
of the original fabric have been isolated and adapted in
each of these three canvases. You might like to try
your hand at creating a fourth design, with the second
pair of birds reversed, back to back, and a flower
motif in the centre.

Strawberry Thief can be used for fitted cushions,
chair seats or stools as you can easily adapt the pro-
portions by working more or less background (see
page 105). If you have difficulty deciding which of the
'thieves' you prefer, they work very well as a complementary set!

I was drawn to the large flowers between the birds
in *Strawberry Thief I*. This was much more challeng-
ing than *Trellis*, my first project (page 37), and I
wanted to try a three-dimensional object. I felt guilty
about straying from Morris's original, and it took
some thought before I could decide what had to be
omitted. I could have left some leaves under the birds'
tails, but they were not growing from anywhere logical so I left them out. Some of the finer foliage also
had to be omitted as it would not have shown clearly
when stitched.

After several drawings and experimental stitching
sessions, I was reasonably happy. I had to blend two
shades of wool in the needle for the markings on the
birds and the seeds in the flowers, to prevent them

looking harsh and unnatural. The heavy outlines on the original fabric would have looked clumsy in tent stitch, so shading was used to achieve the same effect without straying too far from the original.

Strawberry Thief I was not an ideal shape for a chair seat: chairs are usually wider at the front. The second pair of birds in the original Morris print, however, sit conveniently above flowers which extend beyond them, so I used them for *Strawberry Thief II*. The colours are, for the most part, the same as the first *Strawberry Thief* design. At first, I was worried that the strawberries would be too bright for many people's houses, but this has proved to be the most popular of the three and I now think this is probably due to the red berries. Almost nothing was omitted from this part of the fabric; it is very true to Morris's original.

The idea of adding a third design to the *Strawberry Thief* set came some time after the first two, after both *Bird* (page 22) and *Bird and Lily* (page 27) had been created. Between the two birds featured in *Strawberry Thief II* is a lovely curving plant, and I do not know why I had not seriously considered it sooner. The whole design in *Strawberry Thief III* has had to be moved together as it was too wide if kept in the same proportion as the other two. The flowers at the base are also not as closely clustered in the original.

Above: Strawberry Thief II looks very handsome on this elegant japanned and gilded chair in Kelmscott Manor. Their chair was shown by Morris & Co. at the London International Exhibition in 1862. It has recently been attributed to the architect Philip Webb.

Right: A perfect example of how to adapt a design for a particular purpose; the bird is taken from *Strawberry Thief II* and *III*. The hassock is one of several made by Jean Wells for the church at Kelmscott Manor, where William Morris is buried.

Far Right: This magnificent 'X' chair adds history as well as drama to *Strawberry Thief I*. It was brought from the East by the Beale family, the original owners of Standen, the house designed and decorated by Philip Webb and William Morris in 1892.

INSTRUCTIONS–Strawberry Thief I

Size
Design area: 155 stitches high × 225 stitches wide
Size of the design: 11 × 16 in (28 × 41 cm)

Materials
14-mesh single canvas, 4 in (10 cm) larger each way than the size of the required worked area, including the background

Size 20 tapestry needle

Appleton's crewel wool:

☐ light pink (221) – 4 skeins

▨ mid pink (222) – 4 skeins

▨ dark pink (223) – 4 skeins

▨ browny-pink (204) – 2 skeins

☐ pale green-blue (642) – 1 skein

▨ dark green-blue (644) – 1 skein

☐ light green (352) – 1 skein

▨ mid green (355) – 4 skeins

▨ dark green (356) – 4 skeins

▨ honey (692) – 1 skein

▨ golden brown (901) – 1 skein

☐ ivory (882) – 4 skeins

Background: indigo blue (926) – 5 hanks, sufficient to extend the background to 15 × 17 in (38 × 43 cm)

Note The background indigo blue is also used for the veins of the greeny blue leaves and the birds' eyes. If you decide to use a different background colour which is not suitable for these details, you will also need 1 skein of indigo blue (926).

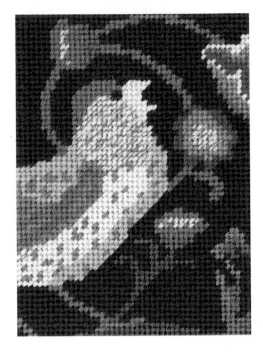

Order of stitching
If you are making a fitted shape, such as a chair seat, you may need a template (see page 104). If you are not using a template, mark out the background.

Fold the canvas in half each way to find the centre. Baste along the fold lines, using coloured sewing thread.

The design is embroidered in tent stitch (see page 106), and the background can be either tent stitch or cashmere stitch (see page 107). Use three threads of wool in the needle throughout. If you like to work with a frame, see page 102.

Start in the centre of the chart, then fill in the design. (Each square represents one stitch.) The speckled areas of the birds' heads, throats and bodies, from the back leg to the tail, are stitched with two threads of ivory to one of golden brown in the needle. Work the centres of the smaller pink flowers with two threads of ivory to one pale green-blue.

Complete the design before stitching the background. If you are using cashmere stitch for the background, you will need to adjust the length of the stitches to fit round the outline of the design.

Above right: The soft speckling on the bird's breast is achieved by blending different colours in the needle.

INSTRUCTIONS–Strawberry Thief II

Size

Design area: 157 stitches high × 189 stitches wide

Size of the design: 11 × 13¹/₂ in (28 × 34 cm)

Materials

14-mesh single canvas, 4 in (10 cm) larger each way than the size of the required worked area, including the background

Size 20 tapestry needle

Appleton's crewel wool:

☐ light pink (221) – 1 skein

▨ dark pink (223) – 1 skein

☐ light green-blue (641) – 1 skein

▨ mid green-blue (642) – 4 skeins

▨ dark green-blue (644) – 1 skein

☐ light green (352) – 2 skeins

▨ mid green (355) – 4 skeins

▨ dark green (356) – 4 skeins

☐ honey (692) – 2 skeins

▨ golden brown (901) – 1 skein

☐ ivory (882) – 4 skeins

▨ scarlet (504) – 2 skeins

Background: indigo blue (926) – 5 hanks, sufficient to extend the background to 15 × 17 in (38 × 43 cm)

Note The background indigo blue is also used for the veins of the greeny blue leaves and the birds' eyes. If you prefer to work with a different background colour, which is not suitable for these details, you will also need 1 skein of blue (926).

Order of stitching

If you are making a fitted shape, such as a chair seat, you may need a template (see page 104). If not, mark out the background area. Fold the canvas in half each way to find the centre. Baste along the fold lines, using bright-coloured sewing thread. The design is embroidered in tent stitch (see page 106), and the background can be either tent stitch or cashmere stitch (see page 107). Use three threads of wool in the needle throughout. If you like to work with a frame, see pages 102–3.

Find the centre of the chart and count from there to one of the strawberries on either side. (Each square on the chart represents one stitch.) Stitch the strawberries first and continue stitching the design out from the centre.

For the body of each bird, use two threads of ivory and one of honey in the needle to give a finely speckled effect (see page 16).

Complete the design before stitching the background. If you are using cashmere stitch for the background, you will need to adjust the length of the stitches to fit round the outline of the design.

Note: Wings are stitched in light and mid-green blue, leaves at base in mid- and dark-green blue with background blue veins. The centre of the base of the design is filled with 642.

INSTRUCTIONS–Strawberry Thief III

Size

Design area: 159 stitches high × 225 stitches wide

Size of the design: $11^{1}/_{2} \times 16$ in (29 × 41 cm)

Materials

14-mesh single canvas, 4 in (10 cm) larger each way than the size of the required worked area, including the background

Size 20 tapestry needle

Appleton's crewel wool:

- ☐ light pink (221) – 1 skein
- ■ dark pink (223) – 1 skein
- ☐ light green-blue (641) – 1 skein
- ☐ mid green-blue (642) – 4 skeins
- ☐ dark green-blue (644) – 1 skein
- ☐ light green (352) – 4 skeins
- ■ mid green (355) – 4 skeins
- ■ dark green (356) – 4 skeins
- ☐ honey (692) – 4 skeins
- ■ golden brown (901) – 1 skein
- ☐ ivory (882) – 4 skeins
- ■ scarlet (504) – 1 skein

Background: indigo blue (926) – 5 hanks, sufficient to extend the background to 15 × 17 in (38 × 43 cm)

Note The background indigo blue is also used for the veins of the greeny blue leaves and the birds' eyes. If you decide to work with a different background colour which is not suitable for these details, you will also need 1 skein of blue (926).

Above: I couldn't resist putting my *Strawberry Thief III* cushion in amongst the young strawberry plants in the garden at Kelmscott Manor.

Order of stitching

If you are making a fitted shape, such as a chair seat, you may need a template (see page 104). If you are not, mark out the background area.

Fold the canvas in half each way to find the centre. Baste along the fold lines, using coloured sewing thread.

The design is embroidered in tent stitch (see page 106) and the background in tent stitch or cashmere stitch (see page 107). Use three strands of wool in the needle throughout. If you like to work with a frame, see pages 102–3.

Find the centre of the chart, between the leaves, and count to the nearest leaf. (Each square on the chart represents one stitch.) For the body of each bird, use two threads of ivory and one of honey in the needle, to give a finely speckled effect. For the centre of the small pink flowers, combine one thread of dark green-blue with one of ivory in the needle. For the large central flowers at the top, surround the blue seeds at the base with stitches worked with two threads of honey and one of ivory.

Complete the design before stitching the background. If you are using cashmere stitch, you will need to adjust the length of the stitches to fit round the outline of the design.

Note: The main colour in the central top flower and birds' wings is 641. The green-blue leaves are in 642, 644 with background blue veins.

21

BIRD

*S*trawberry Thief proved so popular that my customers began asking for other bird designs so that they could complete sets of chair covers. William Morris produced many designs incorporating birds, but this one seemed to offer a natural chair seat shape without altering the original design too much. However, there were problems. I had seen a partially painted drawing by Morris, showing two brightly coloured birds and green leaves. The finished tapestries, however, had a very dark blue background, with flat-looking leaves in a lighter blue, and some in light green.

When I tried stitching this combination on canvas, it simply didn't work. Morris's hangings, beautiful as they are, rely largely on their texture. I also wanted a design that would complement *Strawberry Thief*. I compromised and introduced a few shades that were closer to my earlier designs. I made the birds as bright as in the original painting, and the flowers pink and white. I am still unhappy with the orb, or pomegranate, between the birds – it is not as pretty as the original. One day I will work on it a little more.

Right: This chaise longue in the Green Room at Kelmscott Manor is covered in the original *Bird* fabric, which you can see has a larger design than my cushion. In the background is a De Morgan tile, designed for the P&O liner 'India' in 1896.

Below: Bird was William Morris's first woven hanging to include birds. It was originally designed to hang in the drawing room at Kelmscott House, Morris's town house in Hammersmith, West London.

INSTRUCTIONS–Bird

Size

Design area: 143 stitches high × 201 stitches wide

Size of the finished design: $13^{1}/_{2} × 10^{1}/_{2}$ in $(34 × 27$ cm)

Size of the finished cushion: $15^{1}/_{2} × 15^{1}/_{2}$ in $(39.5 × 39.5$ cm)

Materials

14-mesh single canvas, 4 in (10 cm) larger each way than the size of the required worked area, including the background

Size 20 tapestry needle

Appleton's crewel wool:

☐   pale yellow (471) – 1 skein

▨   autumn yellow (473) – 1 skein

▨   pale pastel pink (877) – 2 skeins

▨   mid pink (222) – 2 skeins

▨   dark pink (223) – 2 skeins

▨   light green (401) – 4 skeins

▨   light blue-green (642) – 4 skeins

▨   mid blue-green (644) – 1 skein

▨   darkest blue-green (645) – 2 skeins

▨   turquoise (522) – 2 skeins

▨   mid slate blue (155) – 2 skeins

Background: dark blue (926) – 4 hanks, sufficient to extend the background to approximately. $15^{1}/_{2} × 15^{1}/_{2}$ in $(39.5 × 39.5$ cm).

Note The background dark blue is also used for the birds' eyes. If a different colour is chosen, which is not suitable for this detail, you will also need 1 skein of dark blue (926). Alternatively, you may like to experiment with one of the blue-greens or the turquoise.

Above: Bird made up as a cushion. Piping of a toning shade helps to frame the design.

Chart opposite: For instructions on working the other three-quarters of this symmetrical design see pages 104–5.

Order of stitching

If you are making a fitted design, such as a chair seat, you will need to use a template (see page 104). If not, mark out the background area.

Fold the canvas in half each way to find the centre. Baste along the fold lines with bright-coloured sewing thread.

The whole canvas can be embroidered in tent stitch (see page 106). Use three strands of wool in the needle throughout. If you wish to work with a frame, see pages 102–3.

Find the centre of the chart, in the small flower, and stitch this flower first. (Each square on the chart represents one stitch.) From here, you can either work upwards along the leaves to the pomegranate or complete the leaves below. Always work out from the centre. Complete the design before stitching the background.

The seed effect in the centre of the pomegranate is achieved by blending two strands of light blue-green with one of dark blue in the needle.

Around the turquoise spots on the birds' breasts is a speckled effect, obtained by blending two strands of pale pastel pink and one of mid pink in the needle. The spots on the tops of the birds' wings are also surrounded by speckling, using two strands of pale pastel pink with one of pale turquoise. To create the gleam in the birds' eyes, overstitch one of the dark blue stitches in each eye in pastel pink.

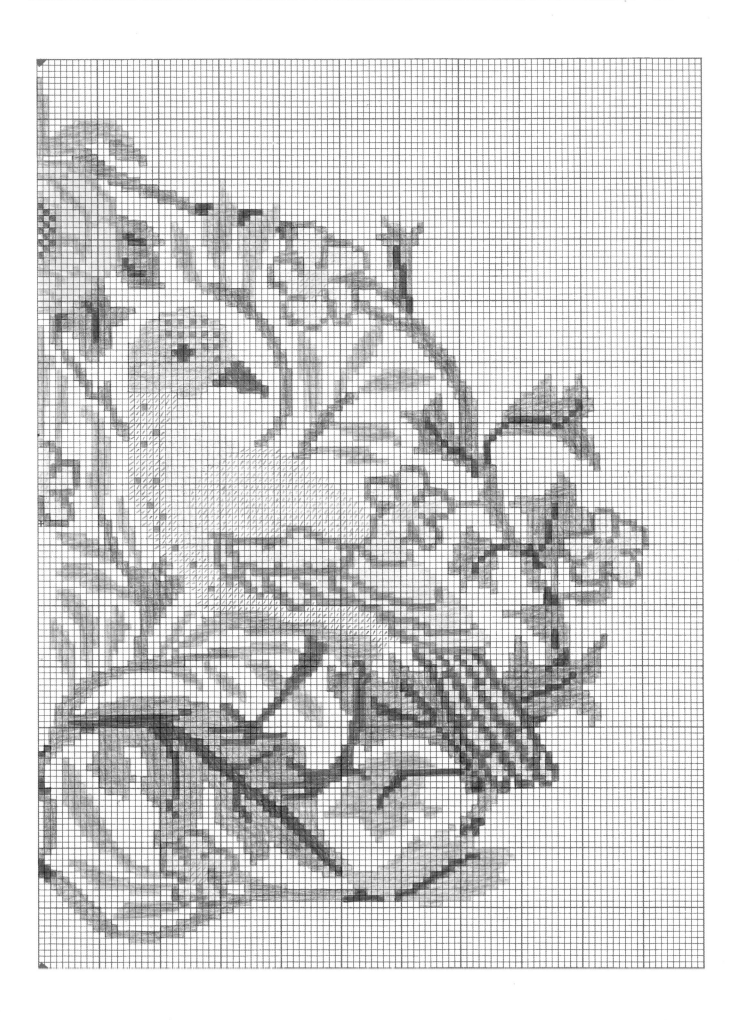

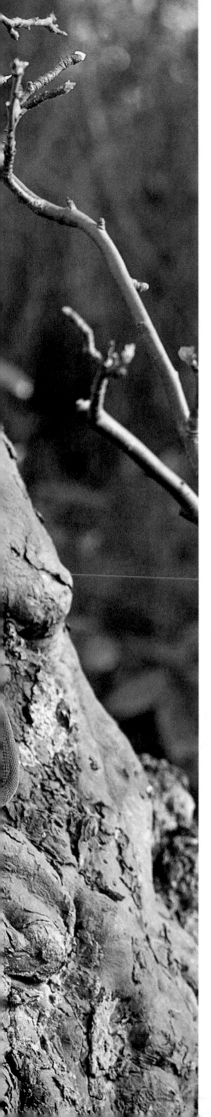

Bird
AND LILY

This was another attempt to satisfy the demand for a set of 'bird' chair seats. Although it is not taken directly from William Morris, there are elements of his style – in the lily, for example. The 'feel' of *Bird and Lily* is also Morris; perhaps slightly less detailed but a clear, strong design which works well with the other 'bird' patterns.

There were no problems with this design. I asked Phyllis Steed, the artist who line draws most of my sketches, to produce a new bird in the same mode as the others. We chose the colours together, I stitched sample areas to see how they would work, and a new design was born.

Far left: Bird and Lily tucked comfortably in one of the remaining apple trees from the original orchard at the Red House in Bexleyheath, Kent. The orchard was already established when Philip Webb built the house for William and Janey Morris as their first home in 1860.

Left: This design is a good choice to soften a Gothic-style chair.

INSTRUCTIONS–Bird and Lily

Size

Design area: 163 stitches high × 219 stitches wide

Size of the finished design: $11^1/_2$ × $15^1/_2$ in (29.5 × 39 cm)

Size of the cushion: $13^1/_2$ × $17^1/_2$ in (33 × 43 cm); size of the chair seat: $17^1/_2$ × 17 in (43.5 × 45 cm)

Materials

14-mesh single canvas, 4 in (10 cm) larger each way than the size of the required worked area, including the background

Size 20 tapestry needle

Appleton's crewel wool:

- ☐ light blue-green (641) – 1 skein
- ▦ mid blue-green (642) – 1 skein
- ▦ dark blue-green (644) – 1 skein
- ▦ light green (352) – 4 skeins
- ▦ mid green (355) – 4 skeins
- ▦ dark green (356) – 4 skeins
- ▦ light yellow (692) – 1 skein
- ▦ light pink (221) – 4 skeins
- ▦ dark pink (223) – 4 skeins
- ▦ browny pink (204) – 4 skeins
- ☐ ivory (882) – 4 skeins

Background: dark blue (926) – 5 hanks, sufficient to extend the background to approx. 13 × 17 in (33 × 43 cm)

Note The background dark blue is also used for the birds' eyes and the seeds of the lily. If a different background colour is chosen, which is not suitable for these details, you will also need 1 skein of dark blue (926).

Order of stitching

If you are making a fitted design, such as a chair seat, you will need to use a template (see page 104). If not, mark out the background area.

Fold the canvas in half each way to find the centre. Baste along the fold lines with bright-coloured sewing thread.

The entire canvas can be embroidered in tent stitch (see page 106). You can also fill in the background with another stitch, such as gobelin filling or cashmere stitch (see page 107), which might prove quicker to embroider and gives an interesting texture. Use three strands of thread in the needle throughout except for gobelin filling, where you will need four strands. If you wish to work with a frame, see page 102.

Find the centre of the chart, in the stem of the lily. Stitch this stem first, then complete the rest of the lily. (Each square on the chart represents one stitch.) Work out from the centre.

Complete the design before stitching the background. If you are using gobelin filling or cashmere stitch for the background, you will need to adjust the length of the stitches to accommodate the outline of the design.

Above: The original working drawing for my *Bird and Lily* design, mirrored by a printed canvas from one of my kits.

Chart opposite: For instructions on working the other half of this symmetrical design see page 104-5.

LODDEN

*L*odden is one of William Morris's most complex textile designs. I admire it enormously – it is intricate without looking contrived. It has four distinct centres, intertwined and blended so cleverly that it took me a while to isolate them. I have used the two more dominant sections, and have tried to separate them from the rest of the design without losing the flow and feel of the original.

I was again forced to change some colours. The leaves in Morris's original simply did not convert into needlepoint. I made the leaves a little more natural, so that our eyes and knowledge of plants feed the imagination and create an impression of realistic foliage.

The stems presented a similar problem. In the original several are shown in outline but, unless I used a much finer canvas, this could not be reproduced in needlepoint. The solution was to make the stems green, which went with the more natural leaves of the needlepoint.

The original textile, still sold at Liberty's in London, has a light background, similar to the version shown on the frame below. The needlepoint can be stitched with a dark background, either to match a *Strawberry Thief* set or simply because it is more practical for a chair seat.

Especially for this book, I made a miniature version of *Lodden* to cover a doll's chair (see pages 7 and 105).

Far right: Both versions of *Lodden* in front of the well at the Red House in Bexleyheath, Kent. Architect Philip Webb's use of red brick, from which the house gets its name, seemed very daring at the time.

Right: Just completed, *Lodden I* leans against one of the original apple trees in the garden of the Red House. Over a hundred years old, this tree was there when William Morris and his family lived in the house (1860–5).

INSTRUCTIONS–Lodden I

Size
Design area: 158 stitches high × 197 stitches wide
Size of the finished design: $11^1/_4 \times 14$ in (28.5 × 35.5 cm)
Size of the finished cushion: $11^1/_2 \times 14^1/_2$ in (29 × 37 cm)

Materials
14-mesh single canvas, 4 in (10 cm) larger each way than the size of the required worked area, including the background

Size 20 tapestry needle

Appleton's crewel wool:

- ▨ light bluey pink (221) – 4 skeins
- ▨ mid bluey pink (222) – 1 skein
- ▨ dark bluey pink (223) – 1 skein
- ▨ light browny pink (202) – 4 skeins
- ▨ darker browny pink (204) – 1 skein
- ☐ pale pastel pink (877) – 2 skeins
- ☐ greeny yellow (331) – 2 skeins
- ▨ light green (352) – 4 skeins
- ▨ blue-green (643) – 4 skeins
- ▨ dark grey-green (293) – 4 skeins

Background: *either* dark blue (926) *or* light grey-blue (875) – 2 hanks for a background area of $11^1/_2 \times 14^1/_2$ in (29.5 × 37 cm)

Order of stitching
If you are making a fitted design, such as a chair seat, you will need to use a template (see page 104). If you are not using a template, mark out the background area on the canvas.

Fold the canvas in half each way to find the centre. Baste along the fold lines with bright-coloured sewing thread. If you prefer to work with a frame, see pages 102–3.

The whole canvas can be embroidered in tent stitch (see page 106). Alternatively, you can use cashmere stitch (see page 107) for the background, to give added texture and also for speed of stitching. Use three strands of wool in the needle throughout.

Find the centre of the chart, in the leaf above the large flower. (Each square on the chart represents one stitch.) Stitch the leaf first and then the flower, and continue working outwards from the centre of the design.

Complete the design before stitching the background. If you are using cashmere stitch for the background, you will need to adjust the length of the stitches so that they fit round the outline of the design.

Below: Lodden I and II together in a bedroom at Standen, in East Grinstead. The house was built by Philip Webb and many of the furnishings came from Morris & Co. The *Powdered* wallpaper in the background was reprinted recently by Sanderson's for the National Trust, using Morris's original blocks.

Chart opposite: For instructions on working the other half of this symmetrical design see page 104-5.

INSTRUCTIONS – Lodden II

Size
Design area: 158 stitches high × 195 stitches wide
Size of the finished design: $11^1/4 \times 14$ in $(29 \times 36$ cm$)$
Size of the finished cushion: $11^1/2 \times 14^1/2$ in $(29 \times 37$ cm$)$

Materials
14–mesh single canvas, 4 in (10 cm) larger each way than the size of the required worked area, including background

Right: Lodden I and II made up as a harmonizing pair of cushions, shown on the steps in the idyllic garden at Standen.

Chart opposite: For instructions on working the other half of this symmetrical design see page 104–5.

Size 20 tapestry needle

Appleton's crewel wool:

- ▨ mid bluey pink (222) – 1 skein
- ▨ dark bluey pink (223) – 1 skein
- ▨ light browny pink (202) – 2 skeins
- ▨ darker browny pink (204) – 1 skein
- ☐ pale pastel pink (877) – 2 skeins
- ☐ greeny yellow (331) – 1 skein
- ▨ pale green (352) – 4 skeins
- ▨ dark clear green (354) – 4 skeins
- ▨ blue-green (643) – 4 skeins
- ▨ dark grey-green (293) – 4 skeins

Background: *either* dark blue (926) *or* light grey-blue (875) – 2 hanks if the background area is $11^1/2 \times 14^1/2$ in $(29 \times 37$ cm$)$

Order of stitching
Follow the instructions for *Lodden I*.

TRELLIS

This was the first William Morris design I attempted to adapt, and probably the easiest. It was also Morris's own first wallpaper design, believed to have been inspired by the rose trellis in his garden at the Red House, Bexleyheath, where he spent the early years of his married life (1860–65). I had seen the wallpaper in Sanderson's in London, the perfect square for a cushion. I adore the rigidity of the wood softened by the entwining roses, and the birds (drawn by Philip Webb, the architect of the Red House) add a surprising splash of colour.

Sanderson still produce the hand-blocked *Trellis* wallpaper in two colourways, and at Kelmscott Manor I found yet another version, with yellow roses (see below).

It was a simple matter to reduce the scale to an appropriate cushion size, draw it onto canvas and stitch the colours in to see if they worked. I wanted to give the feel of the wood grain, so I used straight gobelin filling stitch for the trellis itself. The roses are beautiful, and appear in many of Morris's later designs; they are slightly shaded. I was able to match the wallpaper very closely, and it looked exactly as I wanted it to.

Far left: The *Trellis* cushion on William Morris's own chair in the Old Kitchen at Kelmscott Manor, where many of his possessions and designs are displayed.

Left: Another colourway of the *Trellis* design, which I saw at Kelmscott Manor. Sanderson are currently producing two more versions in their hand-blocked range of Morris wallpapers.

INSTRUCTIONS – Trellis

Size

Design area: 200 × 200 stitches
Size of the finished design: $14^1/_4 \times 14^1/_4$ in
(36 × 36 cm)

Note The cushion shown in the photograph has been extended by adding a few rows of the background ivory beyond the trellis, so that it measures 15 × 15 in (38 × 38 cm).

Materials

14-mesh single canvas, 4 in (10 cm) larger each way than the size of the required worked area, including the background

Size 20 tapestry needle

Appleton's crewel wool:

☐   light blue (562) – 1 skein

▨   mid blue (564) – 1 skein

▨   dark blue (565) – 2 skeins

▨   pink (205) – 2 skeins

▨   mid pink (207) – 2 skeins

▨   dark pink (209) – 2 skeins

▨   honey (695) – 1 skein

▨   brown (697) – 1 skein

▨   putty (984) – 1 hank

▨   grey (983) – 4 skeins

▨   light green (352) – 1 hank

▨   dark green (335) – 1 hank

Background: ivory (882) – $1^1/_2$ hanks, sufficient to extend the background to approx. $14^1/_4 \times 14^1/_4$ in (36 × 36 cm); if you wish to have a wider border beyond the trellis, you will need more background yarn

38

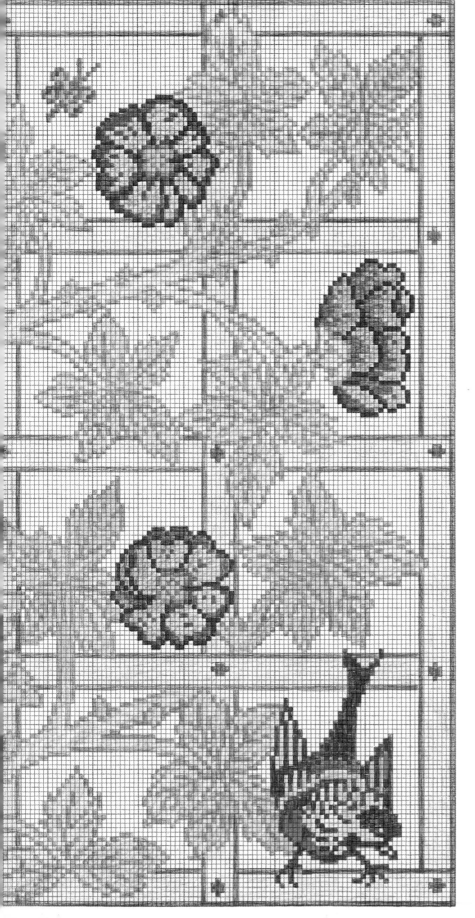

Order of stitching

Fold the canvas in half both ways to find the centre. Baste along the fold lines with bright-coloured sewing thread. You may find the design easier to stitch if you draw in the lines of the trellis on the canvas with a *hard* pencil, and use these grid lines for reference.

The design is embroidered in tent stitch (see page 106), except for the trellis itself which is embroidered in gobelin filling (see page 107). For tent stitch, use three strands of wool in the needle. For gobelin filling, use four strands. If you wish to work with a frame, see page 102–3.

Find the centre of the chart, at the central nail of the trellis. Count out to the nearest leaf shape and stitch this first, then work outwards from the centre of the design. (Each square on the chart represents one stitch.) Stitch the design first, then the nails, then the trellis and then the background.

The trellis

As gobelin filling is a straight rather than a diagonal stitch, it lies between the canvas threads rather than over them. It would appear from the chart that there are two rows of outline grey and six rows of putty in between. In fact, you will find there is room for seven rows of putty. The trellis consists of nine rows in all.

The direction of the stitches on the trellis should be the same, horizontal or vertical, as the relevant portion of trellis. Where one length of trellis passes behind another piece, or where the design lies on top of the trellis, you will need to shorten some stitches so that they appear to pass underneath.

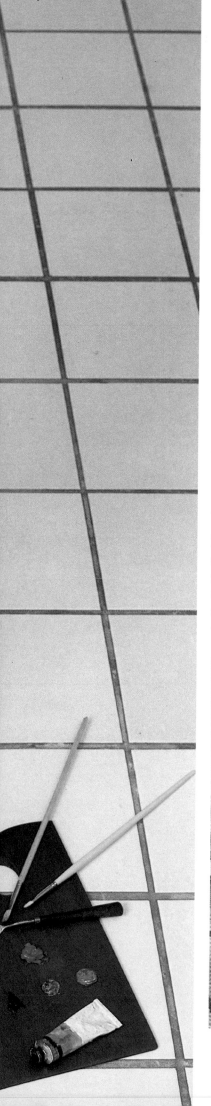

TIFFANY WINDOW

This design is taken from a section of a fabulous domed skylight made about 1900 by the famous American glass artist Louis Comfort Tiffany (1848–1933). Son of Charles Tiffany, the founder of Tiffany & Co., he was known for his iridescent stained glass and the famous 'Favrile' lamps of the 1890s. How I envy the owner of the house who commissioned such a work of art for his garden room!

Only part of the circular design could be used, so I have shortened the branches to bring the two groups of leaves and flowers closer together. I think the leading round the flowers works well, and the shading of the sky. We have nearly achieved the iridescence of the original, with its feeling of light penetrating the white clouds.

Far left: This dramatic photograph of *Tiffany Window* accentuates the strong lines and angles of this unusual design.

Left: When it comes to stitching the sky, feel free to blend the colours of the sky and clouds as you wish – 'painting' in thread is fun!

INSTRUCTIONS – Tiffany Window

Size

Design area: 203 stitches high × 217 stitches wide

Size of the completed 'window': $11^3/4 \times 12$ in $(30 \times 30.5$ cm$)$

Materials

18-mesh single canvas, 4 in (10 cm) larger each way than the size of the required worked area, including the background

Size 22 tapestry needle

Appleton's crewel wool:

- ☐ white (991) – 2 skeins
- ☐ yellow (553) – 1 skein
- ☐ lighter grey (974) – 1 skein
- ■ dark grey (976) – 1 hank
- ▨ lightest green (543) – 1 skein
- ▨ light mid green (544) – 1 skein
- ▨ dark mid green (545) – 1 skein
- ▨ darkest green (547) – 1 skein
- ▨ blue-green (402) – 1 skein
- ☐ yellowy green (251) – 1 skein
- ▨ light brown (764) – 1 skein
- ■ dark brown (304) – 1 skein
- ▨ light turquoise (564) – 1 skein
- ▨ dark turquoise (488) – 1 skein

For sky:

cream (882) – 1 hank
pale blue (562) – 2 hanks
pastel blue (875) – 1 hank

'Frame': biscuit (762) and golden brown (901) – 1 hank of each, sufficient to make a border $1^1/4$ in (3 cm) all round the design

Order of stitching

The entire canvas can be filled with tent stitch (see page 106), but it looks attract-ive if the sky is worked in gobelin filling (see page 107). Use two strands of wool in the needle for tent stitch, and three for gobelin filling.

Fold the canvas in half each way to find the centre. Baste along the fold lines with bright-coloured sewing thread. If you like to work with a frame, see pages 102–3.

Find the centre of the chart, which is in the sky. Do not stitch this yet; instead, count from here either to the branch above or to the leaves on either side, and stitch these. (Each square on the chart represents one stitch.) Complete the rest of the design before stitching the sky.

The shading of the sky is achieved by using three strands of wool in the needle and varying the colours, using gobelin filling horizontally over four threads of canvas. Start with the solid cream cloud in the centre (marked in outline on the chart). Make sure that the edges of all the clouds are not too straight. Com-plete the rest of the sky, radiating out-wards from the cream and changing the colours by mixing the wools in the needle. Use the photograph on page 41 for reference, but let the configuration of the clouds be your own choice. The possible variations are 3 cream; 2 cream and 1 pastel blue; 1 cream and 2 pastel blue; 3 pastel blue; 2 pastel blue and 1 pale blue; 1 pastel blue and 2 pale blue; and 3 pale blue.

If you prefer to use tent stitch, the same principle of colour mixing applies, but as you can only comfortably use two threads in the needle there is less scope for shading.

If you are using gobelin filling for the sky, adjust the length of the stitches to fit round the outline of the design.

For the 'frame' round the finished design, blend two strands of biscuit with one of golden brown in the needle and work in gobelin filling. *Tiffany Window* can be used on a table top or workbox, or framed.

Wild Flowers

I first saw the *Celandine* wallpaper, originally designed for Morris & Co. by Henry Dearle, at Sanderson's. The colours are flat – no shading – and the flowers simplistic. Here were four matching designs for a set of chair seats.

I began by drawing the wreath of leaves on canvas; the simplicity of the flowers dictated the choice of 13-mesh canvas. The wallpaper uses the same greens for the wreath and the leaves of the flowers, but I decided to add olive greens in the centre.

I was worried at first about the practicality of the cream background colour, so I chose three darker shades to tone with the flowers. If you look closely at the photographs showing the different background colours, you will notice that each embroiderer picked out a slightly different dividing line between the inner and outer background!

In the end, I prefer the ivory shade. So the original colour wins.

Far right: The complete set of four *Wild Flowers* designs, used in different ways. The framed picture on the wall is *Celandine*, the cushions are *Primula* (left) and *Bluebell* (right), and the chair seat is *Harebell*.

Right: William Morris's *Celandine* wallpaper was the inspiration for my *Wild Flowers* designs. Sanderson are currently producing two versions in their hand-blocked range of Morris wallpapers.

INSTRUCTIONS – Wild Flowers

Size

Design area: 193 stitches high × 196 stitches wide

Size of the finished design: 14³/₄ × 15 in (37.5 × 38 cm)

Size of the finished cushion: 16 × 16 in (41 × 41 cm)

Materials

14-mesh single canvas, 4 in (10 cm) larger each way than the size of the required worked area, including the background

For each design
Size 20 tapestry needle

Appleton's crewel wool:

☐   ivory (882) – 1 hank

☐   lightest green (542) – 1 hank

☐   mid green (544) – 4 skeins

☐   darker green (547) – 4 skeins

☐   dark grey-green (294) – 4 skeins

☐   dark olive green (244) – 1 skein

☐   mid olive green (242) – 1 skein

Background: choose from maroon (209), blue (321), ivory (882) *or* gold (694) – 5 hanks, sufficient to extend the background to approx. 16 × 16 in (41 × 41 cm) if you are using gobelin filling; cashmere stitch and tent stitch will cover a slightly smaller area

plus
Harebell (right)

☐   light olive green (241) – 1 skein

☐   lighter blue (561) – 1 skein

☐   darker blue (565) – 1 skein

Order of stitching

If you are making a fitted design, such as a chair seat, you will need to use a template (see page 104). If you are not using a template, mark out the background area.

The whole canvas can be executed in tent stitch (see page 106). Alternatively, you might prefer to use tent stitch for the ivory background round the flowers within the wreath, and gobelin filling or brick stitch (page 107) for the outer background, to add to the texture and interest. Use three strands of wool in the needle throughout for tent stitch, and four for gobelin filling and brick stitch.

Fold the canvas in half both ways to find the centre. Baste along the fold lines with bright-coloured sewing thread.

Find the centre of the chart and count from there to the nearest flower. (Each square on the chart represents one stitch.) Start stitching the flower, and continue working outwards from the centre of the design. Complete the wreath of leaves before stitching the inner background in tent stitch.

If you are using gobelin filling or brick stitch for the outer background, you will need to adjust the length of the stitches to accommodate the outline of the design.

Below: As luck would have it, the bluebells were in flower in the garden at Standen the day we were there. Wild flowers were an important source of design for much of William Morris's work in textiles.

Bluebell

lighter blue (743) – 1 skein

dark blue (746) – 1 skein

yellow (474) – 1 skein

and the seven colours listed on page 47, plus background

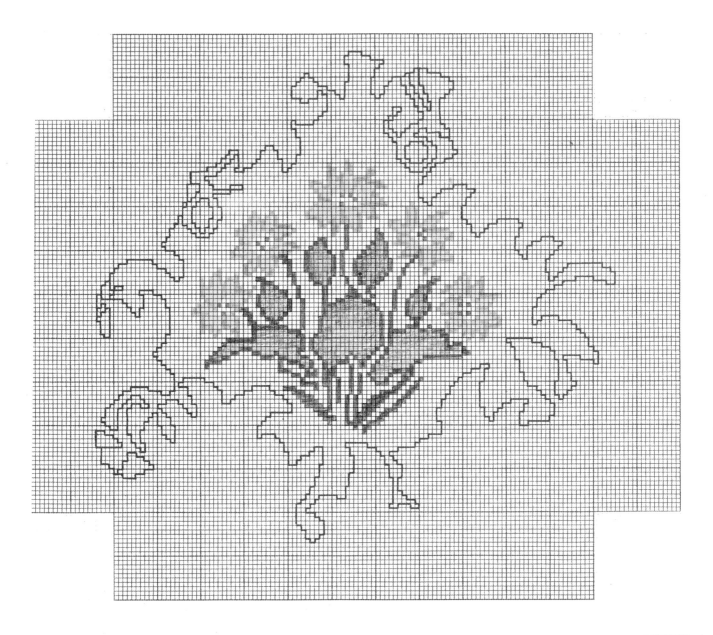

Celandine

- light olive green (241) – 1 skein
- light yellow (471) – 1 skein
- deep yellow (473) – 1 skein

and the seven colours listed on page 47, plus background

Primula

☐   light olive green (241) – 1 skein

▨   light pink (221) – 1 skein

▨   deep pink (223) – 1 skein

and the seven colours listed on page 47, plus background

TULIPS AND DAFFODILS

A few years ago, I visited an exhibition of G. P. & J. Baker's fabrics at the Victoria and Albert Museum in London. The two brothers, sons of a merchant trading out of Turkey, were contemporaries of William Morris, and their company laid great emphasis on design. Their printed fabrics were strongly influenced by Turkish and Persian textiles, and their stylized floral patterns have remained immensely popular.

Two of their designs, both from the late 1890s, attracted me. *Lynham* has very stylized tulips growing from behind large, unrelated leaves, with a gorgeous swirling background. I knew I could not reproduce the background on canvas, and there was no small section of the design that made sense by itself – it needed to be seen as a large repeating pattern. Nevertheless, I still wanted to use the tulips.

Fortunately, I saw another design, *Garden of Tulips*, with more realistic tulip heads but strange wobbly leaves. I thought I could swirl them into a circle, and

Far right: A host of golden daffodils! Choose between two different backgrounds – the stark contrast of the delicate flowers against the dark green, or the pale and pretty effect of the light green background.

Right: This version of *Tulips* has a mid Prussian blue background (Appleton's 324). An alternative background colourway is shown overleaf.

Right: The *Tulips* cushion on the windowsill at Kelmscott Manor. The modern Thai carving perfectly complements the style of the Arts and Crafts era.

keep the head of the tulip from the first design (which was much easier to transfer to canvas) and the 'feel' of the other.

I sketched it, and my artist outlined it. To stitch all the heads in one set of colours would have been tedious, so I marked out two tulip head colours in two groups of yellows. When the design was finally stitched, and we could see it worked well, I chose two sets of pinks as an alternative (see page 54).

If neither of these fits in with your room setting, it would be a simple matter to create further colour schemes, based on natural tulip shades, for example a blend of whites and creams, or of different shades of red or purple.

The original of *Daffodils* was a black and white drawing I saw briefly at an exhibition in Hampstead, north London. Done in the early 1900s, it showed swirling daffodils. One normally thinks of daffodils as very straight and upright flowers – as, to start with, are tulips. I decided a companion to *Tulips* would be pretty, and I think they work very well together – I hope you agree.

Below: This yellow *Tulips* colourway echoes the window so prettily. The stained glass was commissioned by William Morris when he first moved into the Red House at Bexleyheath, and is found on the upper landing there.

INSTRUCTIONS – Tulips

Size

Design area: 253 stitches high × 264 stitches wide

Size of the finished design: 14 × 14$^{1}/_{2}$ in (35.5 × 37 cm)

Size of the finished cushion: 15 × 15 in (38 × 38 cm)

Materials:

18-mesh single canvas, 4 in (10 cm) larger each way than the size of the required worked area, including the background

Size 22 tapestry needle

Appleton's crewel wool:

Pink tulips

☐ A light bluey pink (751) – 1 skein

◩ B mid bluey pink (754) – 1 skein

◼ C dark bluey pink (755) – 1 skein

▨ D pastel pink (877) – 2 skeins

◼ E mid browny pink (222) – 1 skein

◼ F dark browny pink (223) – 1 skein

☐ G white (991B) – 1 skein

▨ H light green (352) – 1 hank

◩ I mid green (354) – 4 skeins

◼ J dark green (547) – 1 skein

Background: ivory (882) or blue (324) – 3 hanks, sufficient to extend the background to 16 × 16 in (41 × 41 cm)

Yellow tulips

A lightest soft yellow (841) – 1 skein

B soft warm yellow (471) – 1 skein

C golden yellow (473) – 1 skein

D palest yellow (872) – 2 skeins

E clear yellow (551) – 1 skein

F light greeny yellow (842) – 1 skein

G white (991B) – 1 skein

H light green (251) – 1 hank

I mid green (242) – 4 skeins

J dark green (244) – 1 skein

Background: dark blue (324) – 3 hanks, sufficient to extend the background to 16 × 16 in (41 × 41 cm)

Order of stitching

If you are making a fitted design, you will need to make a template. If not, mark out the background on the canvas.

The entire canvas may be embroidered in tent stitch with two strands of thread throughout. You may choose to fill in the background with another, such as cashmere stitch or gobelin filling which might prove quicker and would create an interesting texture. In this case, you may find that you need an extra thread of wool to cover the canvas completely.

Fold the canvas in half both ways to find the centre. Baste along the fold lines with bright-coloured sewing thread. If you work with a frame, see pages 102–3.

Now find the centre of the chart. (Each square on the chart represents one stitch.) Work out from the centre and complete the design before stitching the background.

If using cashmere stitch or gobelin filling for the background, you will need to adjust the length of the stitches to fit round the outline of the design.

INSTRUCTIONS – Daffodils

Size
Design area: 252 stitches high × 231 stitches wide
Size of the finished design: 14 × 13 in (36 × 33 cm)
Size of the finished cushion: 15 × 15 in (38 × 38 cm)

Materials
18-mesh single canvas, 4 in (10 cm) larger each way than the size of the required worked area, including the background

Size 22 tapestry needle

Appleton's crewel wool:

☐ cream (871) – 2 skeins

☐ creamy yellow (841) – 1 skein

☐ clear bright yellow (551) – 1 skein

☐ deep yellow (552) – 1 skein

▨ deepest yellow (553) – 1 skein

▨ orangey yellow (474) – 1 skein

▨ dark greeny yellow (842) – 2 skeins

▨ lighter fawn (761) – 1 skein

■ darker fawn (901) – 1 skein

☐ light yellowy green (543) – 1 skein

▨ light green (401) – 1 hank

▨ dark green (403) – 4 skeins

▨ deepest green (406) – 1 skein

Background: light green (873) *or* dark green (296) – 3 hanks, sufficient to extend the background to 15 × 15 in (38 × 38 cm)

Order of stitching
Follow the instructions for *Tulips* (see page 56).

All the outlines of leaves and the stamens of the flowers are worked in dark green (403). The outer sides of the leaves and the stamen heads are light green (401). The undersides of the leaves are light yellowy green (543). The leaf veins are stitched in deepest green (406). The petals and veins of all the flowers and the trumpets of the lighter flowers are outlined in dark greeny yellow (842). The trumpet outline of the darker flowers is orangey yellow (474). The petals of the darker flowers are clear bright yellow (551).

The inner trumpet of the darker flowers is deepest yellow (553), while their outer trumpets and the underside of their petals are deep yellow (552). The petals of the lighter flowers are cream (871) and the outer trumpets and undersides of the petals of the lighter flowers are creamy yellow (841).

MAGPIES

The first time I saw this William De Morgan tile was in a black and white photograph. The way the birds are partially concealed behind the leaves was reminiscent of the Brangwyn panels that had entranced me as a child (see the endpapers).

I failed to find the original tile, so I was not sure of De Morgan's colours. But, as he and William Morris worked together, it did not seem unreasonable to stick to Morris's shades (see *Magpies I* below).

I have now seen the original *Magpies* tile, and I am afraid the birds do not remotely resemble mine in colouring – I hope De Morgan will forgive me. I have since developed a new colour scheme, *Magpies II*, with green leaves and a light background, shown left. It illustrates the way in which a good design is capable of different interpretations.

The design echoes the original tile in filling the entire area, but for a cushion it might be better to extend the background area round the design or to frame it with a border, using some of the design colours.

Far left: My new colourway, *Magpies II*, shown half completed on a frame. I like to think that the partially worked embroidery and the outline of the design are reminiscent of William Morris's delicate working drawings. This alcove setting is in the first floor drawing room at the Red House, Bexleyheath, where the light is ideal for embroidery.

Left: The first *Magpies* colour scheme, *Magpies I*, handsomely framed.

61

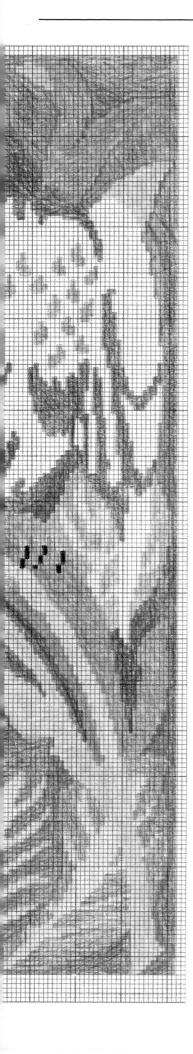

INSTRUCTIONS – Magpies

Size
Design area: 202 stitches high × 202 stitches wide
Size of the finished design: 14¼ × 14¼ in (36 × 36 cm)

Materials
14-mesh single canvas, 4 in (10 cm) larger each way than the required worked area, including the background

Size 20 tapestry needle

Appleton's crewel wool:
Magpies I (opposite)

☐	A	white (991) – 1 hank
☐	B	ivory (882) – 1 hank
☐	C	yellowy green (331) – 4 skeins
☐	D	dark honey (695) – 1 skein
☐	E	light grey (151) – 1 skein
■	F	dark browny grey (976) – 1 hank
■	G	lighter pink (204) – 1 hank
■	H	darker pink (205) – 1 hank
☐	I	light green (352) – 4 skeins
■	J	blue-green (642) – 4 skeins
■	K	black (993) – 1 skein

Background: dark blue (926) – 1 hank

Magpies II

	A	white (991B) – 1 hank
	B	light green (251A) – 4 skeins
	C	mid green (251) – 4 skeins
	D	yellow (474) – 1 skein
	E	light grey (151) – 1 skein
	F	dark grey (965) – 1 hank
	G	darker green (255) – 1 hank
	H	darkest green (256) – 1 hank
	I	light brown (764) – 1 hank
	J	dark brown (766) – 4 skeins
	K	black (993) – 1 skein

Background: ivory (882) – 1 hank

Order of stitching
The whole design can be worked in tent stitch, using three strands of wool.

Fold the canvas in half both ways to find the centre. Baste along the fold lines with bright-coloured sewing thread. If you work with a frame, see pages 102–3.

Find the centre of the chart, in the central leaf, and stitch outwards from there. Each square on the chart represents one stitch. Complete the design before stitching the background.

Apart from the colour changes, the two versions of *Magpies* are much the same, but there is one difference. All the leaf veins are the same colour (ivory) in *Magpies I*. In *Magpies II* the leaf veins are in two different colours: the lighter green leaves (which correspond to the yellowy green leaves (331) of *Magpies I*) have light brown veins.

HOLLAND PARK

William Morris's name for this handsome design was *Carbrook*, a hand-tufted carpet produced by 'the Firm' more than once. Alexander Ionides commissioned the carpet from Morris & Co. for the Antiquity Room in his house at No. 1, Holland Park, West London, in 1883, and it is now in the Victoria and Albert Museum in London. I used to refer to the design as *Holland Park* when I was working on it and the name stuck.

Before seeing the original Ionides carpet, I had been working on a brown colour scheme as I had already produced several designs in blue. I had only seen a black and white photograph of the original, so it was interesting to find that the colours I had chosen were very similar, except the original has a blue background. It is as well I had not seen it previously as the sheer size would have discouraged me from proceeding.

Holland Park, or *Carbrook*, works well on the finer 8-mesh canvas, making a rug 48 × 27 in (1m 22 cm × 69 cm). It looks equally elegant if the design colours are modified to suit a blue or light grey background. You could also isolate part of the central panel to make a carpet bag, again using the 8-mesh canvas and one thread of Appleton's tapestry wool.

Far left: Set in William Morris's own bedroom at Kelmscott Manor, the *Holland Park* rug in a brown colourway sits well on top of a *Daisy* or *Grass* carpet designed by Morris and woven by Wilton in the 1870s. Jane Morris's "Si je puis" embroidery on the bedspread echoes her husband's "If I can" on his own embroidered wall hanging in the Green Room.

Left: A blue version of the *Holland Park* design.

INSTRUCTIONS – Holland Park Rug

Size
Design area: 371 stitches wide × 205 stitches long
Size of the finished rug: 61 × 34 in (155 × 85 cm)

Materials
6-mesh rug canvas, 6 in (15 cm) larger each way than the size of the required worked area, including the background

Size 16 tapestry needle

Appleton's tapestry wool:

- ▨ lightest browny pink (121) – 7 hanks

- ▨ light mid browny pink (122) – 4 hanks

- ▨ dark mid browny pink (124) – 4 hanks

- ▨ darkest browny pink (126) – 1 hank

- ▨ deep red (209) – 2 hanks, 4 skeins

- ▨ drab green (333) – 5 hanks

- ▨ light green (352) – 8 hanks

- ▨ darker green (354) – 4 hanks

- ▢ lighter blue (641) – 3 hanks, 4 skeins

- ▨ darker blue (156) – 3 hanks

- ▢ pale honey (691) – 7 hanks

Background: dark brown (976) – 13 hanks
Border background: elephant brown (973) – 10 hanks

Order of stitching
The entire rug is worked in cross stitch (see page 107). Use two threads in the needle throughout.

Fold the canvas in half both ways to find the centre. Baste along the fold lines with bright-coloured sewing thread. If you like to work with a frame, see pages 102–3.

Start with the small central flower at the base of the chart. (Each square on the chart represents one stitch.) Complete all the design areas of the central panel before filling in the background, then stitch the border in the same order. Pay special attention to the borders: the distance between the shapes in the short border is different from that on the long sides.

Finishing
When you have finished the stitching, stretch the rug back into shape, if necessary (see page 108). Trim the edges to leave a 2 in (5 cm) wide border of unworked canvas all round. Back the rug, and add a fringe if desired.

Right: The barn at Kelmscott Manor, Gloucestershire, with a grey version of the *Holland Park* rug in the foreground.

Note: The stems and veins of the leaves in the central panel and the pineapple stems should be worked in darker green (354), see page 64.

ACANTHUS

This intriguing design was inspired by a wall hanging designed by William Morris, which I saw in an exhibition of Arts and Crafts textiles held at the Victoria and Albert Museum in London. Morris had several versions worked in different techniques and colours, but it was the silk embroidered one on page 70 that attracted me.

When I started work on it, it did seem the most impractical design I had ever embarked on. I had to use the finer of the two rug canvases to its full width to fit the design in. I have tried to retain the original colours as well as the design as far as possible. As a commercial kit (my original intention) it seemed a no-hoper, but I just loved it and it is still my favourite design. The shades of pink and green are so close that charting them was a nightmare; I wondered if they were really necessary, but to simplify Morris's original was unthinkable.

The background is a blend of two shades to try to reproduce the colour of the silk as closely as possible. In the rug in the photograph, the border background was worked with three strands of one shade and one of the other, and the centre background in two strands of each shade.

The blue background may not be right for your setting. Almost any dark shade would look effective; I long to see *Acanthus* against a charcoal background.

Far right: An *Acanthus* rug in front of the original kitchen range at Standen. The charming toys, chair and Suffolk cart have recently been found in the attic and belonged to the Beale family. The jardiniere went so well with the rug that I couldn't resist putting it into the photograph.

Right: Acanthus used in a traditional way – as a table covering at Kelmscott Manor.

INSTRUCTIONS – Acanthus

Size
Design area: 503 stitches wide × 289 stitches long. Size of finished rug: 66 × 38¹/₂ in (1m 68 cm × 98.5 cm)

Materials
8-mesh canvas, 6 in (15 cm) larger each way than the required worked area
Size 16 tapestry needle

For the design
Appleton's tapestry wool:

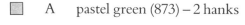	A	pastel green (873) – 2 hanks
	B	light green (874) – 4 hanks
	C	light grey-green (352) – 5 hanks
	D	blue green (401) – 4 hanks
	E	dark grey green (293) – 4 hanks
	F	darkest green (294) – 2 hanks
	G	light greeny yellow (331) – 2 hanks
	H	light olive (241) – 3 hanks
	I	mid olive (242) – 3 hanks
	J	dark olive (244) – 4 skeins
	K	light flesh pink (706) – 2 hanks
	L	clear flesh pink (708) – 1 skein
	M	dark coral pink (204) – 4 skeins
	N	light pink (703) – 1 hank, 4 skeins
	O	light dusky pink (202) – 2 hanks
	P	dark dusky pink (122) – 1 hank, 4 skeins
	Q	cream (881) – 1 hank, 4 skeins
	R	biscuit (762) – 2 hanks
	S	yellow (842) – 4 hanks

For the background
Appleton's crewel wool:

dull blue (324) – 10 hanks

brighter blue (565) – 10 hanks

Order of stitching

Cross stitch (see page 107) is used throughout. Use one thread of tapestry wool in the needle for the design areas. For the background, use four threads of crewel wool: two of dull blue and two of brighter blue. Alternatively, use three strands of one shade and one of the other for the main background, reversing the blend for the border background.

To create a subtly shaded effect, this rug uses a large number of closely related tones of green and pink. Begin by identifying each of your wools on the key. Label each colour with the appropriate code, to avoid confusion when you begin stitching. Refer to the photographs as an additional guide.

Find the centre of the canvas by folding it in half each way. Baste along the fold lines with bright-coloured sewing thread to quarter the design. This corresponds to the centre marks on the charts overleaf.

If you like to work with a frame, see pages 102–3.

Stitch the design before the background. Start by counting from the centre mark on the chart on page 73 to the biscuit-coloured stems, and stitch these first. (Each square on the chart represents one stitch.) Do not worry if, when following the charts, you find some squares where the choice of colours seems to be debatable. Use your own judgment – the general effect is what matters, and it is unlikely that any two rugs will ever be exactly the same.

Finishing

To finish the rug, see page 109.

The colours for the design are used as follows:

A   The veins inside the large acanthus leaves
B   The highlights of the large acanthus leaves and the smaller leaves (mainly on the leaf edges)
C   The shading in the acanthus leaves and the smaller leaves
D   The next shade in the large acanthus and the smaller leaves; the flowers in the border
E   The second darkest shade in the large acanthus; some smaller leaves
F   The darkest shade in the large acanthus leaves
G   The edges of some yellowy green leaves; the flower stems in the border; inside the stems of the four large leaves near the edge of the central panel
H   The lighter colour in the striped leaves; the body of some of the oak leaves; the middle shade of the yellowy leaves in the border
I   The darker shade in the striped leaves; the darkest shade of the yellowy leaves in the border
J   The veins of the small oak leaves
K   The outlines of the small flat orangey flowers; the bell-shaped flowers (central panel only); the lightest shade in the orangey flowers
L   The middle shade in the orangey flowers
M   The darkest shade in the orangey flowers (central panel only)
N   The lightest colour of the border flowers, mainly on the petal tips
O   The middle colour of the border flowers
P   The darkest pink in the border flowers, and in the six bluey pink flowers at the ends of the central panel
Q   The highlights of all the orangey flowers; the main petals of the small flat orangey flowers
R   The stems in the central panel
S   The border turrets; the inner border divider; a few spots in the central panel

Far left: My *Acanthus* needlepoint was inspired by this beautiful silk wall hanging, which is now on display at the Victoria and Albert Museum, London.

HAMMERSMITH

*H*ammersmith as a title for this design is a little confusing, as William Morris used the name for all his hand-tufted carpets. He was attempting at the time to improve the general standard of design in manufactured carpets in Victorian England, and the name *Hammersmith* was used to distinguish between the two.

This design was produced on a loom at Merton Abbey in the early 1900s when Morris was living at Kelmscott House (named after Kelmscott Manor) on the river Thames in Hammersmith, west London. I love the strong simplicity and the traditional colouring. Morris was a great collector of Oriental rugs, which he used as wall hangings. The *Hammersmith* or hand-tufted rugs were individually designed and would have been very costly. They are all works of art.

It was comparatively easy to interpret the main design in cross stitch on coarse canvas. I was forced to omit some fine tracery which would not curve enough and looked too heavy on the canvas. Otherwise the needlepoint looks much like the original. I do, however, keep promising myself that I will knot the fringe as beautifully as that on the *Hammersmith* which inspired me to attempt my first 'carpet'.

Left: The *Hammersmith* design works really well in the simplicity of the beamed attic at Kelmscott Manor. The *Rose Tile* cushion (see page 92), worked in a matching colourway, sits on a chair designed by Rossetti. On the wall hangs a lovely silk embroidery of rose trees.

Below: The original *Hammersmith* rug, showing the fine tracery which, sadly, I had to omit in my needlepoint design.

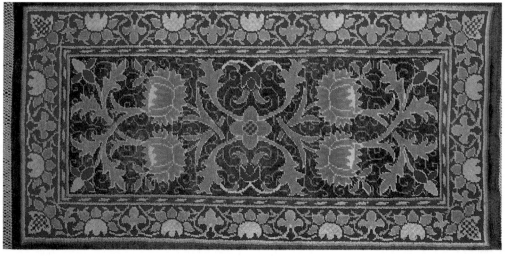

INSTRUCTIONS – Hammersmith

Size

Design area: 325 stitches wide × 165 stitches long

Size of the finished rug: $27\frac{1}{2}$ × 53 in (70 × 135 cm), to include a border of six stitches all round

Materials

6-mesh rug canvas, 6 in (15 cm) larger each way than the size of the required worked area, including the background

Size 16 tapestry needle

Appleton's tapestry wool:

- ☐ beige (984) – 9 hanks
- ☐ light pink (204) – 2 hanks
- ▨ mid pink (206) – 1 hank, 4 skeins
- ■ dark red (227) – 10 hanks
- ■ very dark red (128) – 2 hanks
- ▨ green (342) – 4 hanks, 4 skeins
- ▨ blue-green (293) – 4 hanks
- ▨ light blue (521) – 3 hanks, 4 skeins
- ☐ cream (881) – 4 skeins

Background: dark blue (929) – 13 hanks
Border background: dark red (227) – 10 hanks

Note A band of background dark blue (929), six rows deep, runs around the edge of the rug. As the canvas normally available is 40 in (1 m) wide, it is possible to increase the size of the rug by making this border wider. Allow approx. 2 hanks for three rows all round.

Decide before starting what size rug you want, and buy sufficient canvas and extra wool. You will have enough for six rows of dark blue border with the quantities given.

Order of stitching

The entire rug is worked in cross stitch (see page 107). This creates its own padding and is therefore a hard-wearing stitch. It also causes less distortion of the canvas than many other stitches. Use two threads in the needle throughout.

Fold the canvas in half both ways to find the centre. Baste along the fold lines with bright-coloured sewing thread. If you prefer to work with a frame, see pages 102–3.

Find the centre mark on the chart. (Each square on the chart represents one stitch.) Start with the nine central stitches in dark red, then complete the central shape. Complete all the design before stitching the background.

The background colours have not been coloured in on the chart. The dark blue is the background for the centre of the rug. Note that on the inside of the two large pink flowers there is one stitch where the background encroaches into the design; this stitch is marked in dark blue. Elsewhere in the flowers the plain squares should be worked in cream.

The background of the border is dark red. The very outside of the rug, beyond the three coloured stripes, is again in dark blue.

To finish the rug, see page 109.

*J*ACKFIELD GERANIUM

I n the course of my research into William De Morgan, I came across some beautiful pictorial tiles made by Maw & Co. around 1880. Each has a wide border, with the design overlapping them to give the same sort of three-dimensional effect that I admire in William Morris's *Trellis* (page 37). These strong yet simple designs were ideal for making up into square cushions.

George Maw was one of the first people to use six or more colours in tile production; his experiments with techniques and glazes were so successful that in 1883 he set up a factory at Jackfield in Ironbridge, Shropshire, which in its heyday was producing over 20,000,000 tiles and other ceramics a year, across a range of some 9,000 lines. Among the talented freelance designers that he employed were Walter Crane and Lewis Day, both founder members of the Arts and Crafts Exhibition Society.

The factory has gone, but many of its original products are displayed in a museum on the old site in the Ironbridge Gorge, an area that has been brilliantly restored as a vast open-air museum demonstrating the way that iron, porcelain and other products were made a hundred years ago. It is well worth a visit – you will need at least a day to see it all.

Far right: Jackfield Geranium was taken from a George Maw tile design, and is ideal for a typical Victorian black and gilt frame.

Right: You can achieve subtle effects by creatively blending colours in your needle. For details of the wools used see the diagram on page 80.

INSTRUCTIONS – Geranium Tile

Size
Design area: 201 × 201 stitches
Size of the finished tile: $14^{1}/_{2} \times 14^{1}/_{2}$ in (37 × 37 cm)

Materials
14-mesh single canvas, 4 in (10 cm) larger each way than the size of the required worked area, including the background

Size 20 tapestry needle

Appleton's crewel wool:

- pale coral (861) – 4 skeins
- mid coral (863) – 1 hank
- dark coral (866) – 4 skeins
- light grey (972) – 1 skein
- darker grey (974) – 1 skein
- mauve (456) – 1 skein
- pale yellowy green (251A) – 4 skeins
- grey-green (352) – 4 skeins
- yellowy green (253) – 4 skeins
- darker green (356) – 1 skein
- light yellow (471) – 2 hanks
- dark yellow (474) – 1 hank
- black (993) – 1 hank, 4 skeins
- pastel green (874) – 1 skein

Order of stitching
The entire canvas can be embroidered in tent stitch (see page 106), with three strands of thread in the needle throughout.

Fold the canvas in half both ways to find the centre. Baste along the fold lines with bright-coloured sewing thread. If you prefer to work with a frame, see pages 102–3.

Find the centre of the chart, between the dark leaf and the flowers. Do not stitch the background, but count out from the centre and stitch either the leaf or one of the flowers first. (Each square on the chart represents one stitch.)

Continue working out from the centre of the design. Complete the design before stitching the centre background in black.

For the butterfly, you can experiment with different blends of yarn in the needle – two of one with one of another – to give the shimmery effect of the wings. The diagram below gives details of the different colours blended in the needle for separate sections of the wings. No two butterflies will be exactly alike, but that is the charm of needlepoint and it is fun to do. The main chart gives an overall guide to the colours, so if you prefer you can just use these plain colours.

Surrounding the centre square are two rows of light yellow, followed by two rows of black, before the start of the border. The light yellow forms the background to the border. The whole design is then framed with one row of dark coral.

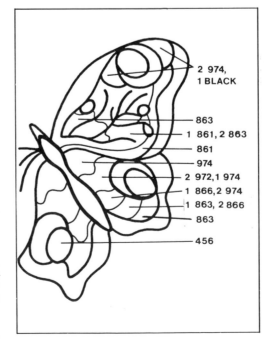

COUNTRY FLOWERS

An exhibition at the Victoria and Albert Museum, London, of fabrics produced by the firm of G.P. and J. Baker inspired this design, and also *Tulips* (page 52).

It is a very traditional pattern, each section containing a flower. The ogival and lozenge shapes run into each other and the overlapping outlines are filled with stylized leaves. I liked the fact that the designs could be neatly finished, and *Spring Flowers* gave me the opportunity to use some wonderfully intertwined daffodils I had seen elsewhere.

The *Spring Flowers* design illustrated features crocuses at the top and bottom. I have also included an optional snowdrop pattern, which you might like to use to replace either the yellow or purple crocuses.

Summer Flowers followed on naturally from *Spring Flowers* and has proved to be more popular, perhaps because of the emphatic poppies. In this case, you could use the extra daisy pattern to add variety.

A lot can be done with this design. My own preference, where *Spring Flowers* is concerned, is for the dark background, which makes the flowers stand out. If you are stitching both designs to make a pair, you could strengthen the colours of *Spring Flowers* to match *Summer Flowers*. You could also emphasize the design by stitching a thicker line of green round the outside to frame it.

The small flowers are useful for a chair seat with a wide front, as they can be added at the bottom only. For a larger stool, you could add a whole section so that there are four tall flowers. This is easily done by extending the lines around the daffodil or poppy to match those that enclose the iris or cornflower. If you need a very long design (perhaps for a fender stool), you could repeat the iris. And if the design is too deep for a chair, then leave out the crocuses or buttercups. There is endless scope for variations – you could even experiment with other flowers.

Right: I've produced two *Country Flowers* designs: *Spring Flowers* (left) and *Summer Flowers* (right). Made up as cushions, they are shown on a tree seat in the front garden at the Red House, Bexleyheath.

Above: An extended version of *Spring Flowers*, worked with a dark background to give the design a completely different feel.

INSTRUCTIONS – Spring Flowers

Size

Design area: 207 stitches high × 201 stitches wide

Size of the finished design: 15 × 14^1/$_2$ in (38 × 37 cm)

Size of the finished cushion: 16 × 16 in (41 × 41 cm)

Size of the finished table-top: 17^1/$_2$ × 17^1/$_2$ in (45 × 45 cm)

Materials

14-mesh single canvas, 4 in (10 cm) larger each way than the size of the required worked area, including the background

Note The cushion design has two small motifs at the top and bottom, but the width may be extended to 16^1/$_2$ in (42 cm) by repeating these motifs, so that you have four at both top and bottom; if you are making this adaptation, you will need canvas 3 in (7.5 cm) wider.

Size 20 tapestry needle

Appleton's crewel wool:

- ▦ light grey-green (352) – 1 skein
- ▦ lighter blue-green (401) – 1 hank
- ▦ darker blue-green (402) – 2 skeins
- ▦ second darkest green (355) – 2 skeins
- ▦ darkest green (356) – 4 skeins
- ▢ yellowy green (543) – 4 skeins
- ▢ palest yellow (872) – 2 skeins
- ▢ bright yellow (553) – 1 skein
- ▢ mid yellow (551) – 2 skeins
- ▦ lightest mauve (884) – 1 skein
- ▦ mid mauve (101) – 1 skein
- ▦ dark mauve (104) – 1 skein
- ▦ pale brown (761) – 1 skein
- ▦ darker brown (763) – 1 skein

Background: lighter pastel grey (875) and darker pastel grey (886) – 2 hanks of each, *or* dark brown (588) – 6 hanks, sufficient to extend the background area to 17^1/$_2$ × 17^1/$_2$ in (45 × 45 cm)

Order of stitching

If you are making a fitted design, such as a chair seat, you will need to use a template (see page 104). If not, mark out the background area.

The whole design can be embroidered in tent stitch (see page 106). Alternatively, use tent stitch for the design and the pale grey background, and cashmere stitch (as shown) or diagonal tent stitch (basketweave) (see pages 106–7) for the darker grey background. Use three strands of wool in the needle throughout.

Fold the canvas in half both ways to find the centre. Baste along the fold lines with bright-coloured sewing thread. If you wish to work with a frame, see pages 102–3.

Find the centre of the chart, in the stem of the iris. Each square on the chart represents one stitch. Start by stitching the iris and work outwards from the centre. Complete the design before stitching the inner background.

If you are using cashmere stitch for the outer background, you will need to adjust the length of the stitches to fit round the outline of the design.

Right: Spring Flowers made up as a cushion.

Chart opposite: For instructions on working the other half of this symmetrical design see page 104–5.

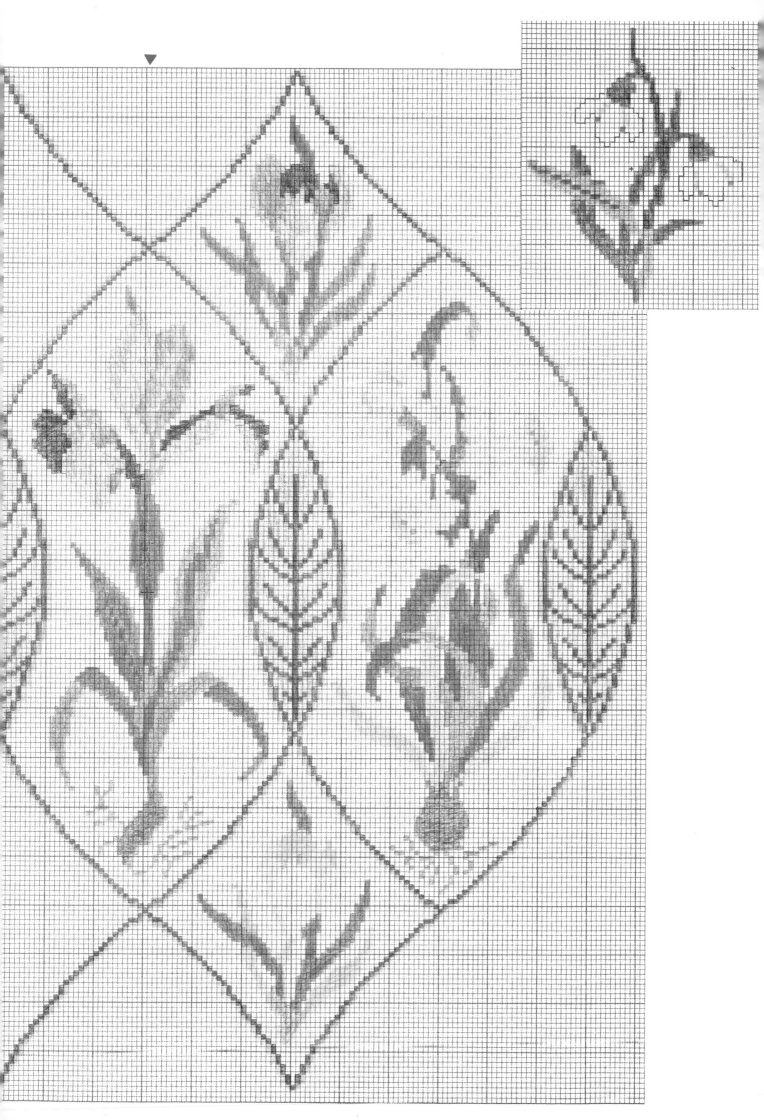

INSTRUCTIONS – Summer Flowers

Size

Design area: 207 stitches deep × 201 stitches wide

Size of the finished design: 15 × 14$\frac{1}{2}$ in (38 × 37 cm)

Size of the finished cushion: 16 × 16 in (41 × 41 cm)

Materials

14-mesh single canvas, 4 in (10 cm) larger each way than the size of the required worked area, including the background

Note The cushion design has two small motifs at the top and bottom, but the width may be extended to 16$\frac{1}{2}$ in (42 cm) by repeating these motifs, so that you have four at both top and bottom (see *Spring Flowers*). If you are making this adaptation, you will need canvas 3 in (7.5 cm) wider.

Size 20 tapestry needle

Appleton's crewel wool:

☐ lightest green (351) – 2 skeins

▨ lightest mid green (542) – 4 skeins

▨ darkest mid green (355) – 1 hank

▨ darkest green (294) – 4 skeins

▨ light orange red (444) – 1 skein

▨ dark orange red (448) – 1 skein

■ darkest red (504) – 1 skein

☐ lightest blue (462) – 1 skein

▨ mid blue (463) – 1 skein

▨ darkest blue (464) – 1 skein

☐ lightest yellow (551) – 1 skein

☐ mid yellow (552) – 1 skein

▨ darkest yellow (553) – 1 skein

▨ pale mauve (602) – 1 skein

■ black (993) – 1 skein

Background: lighter pastel grey (875) and darker pastel grey (886) – 2 hanks of each

Order of stitching

Follow the instructions for *Spring Flowers*. The centre of the *Summer Flowers* design is below the smaller cornflower; count from there to the flower and stitch that first.

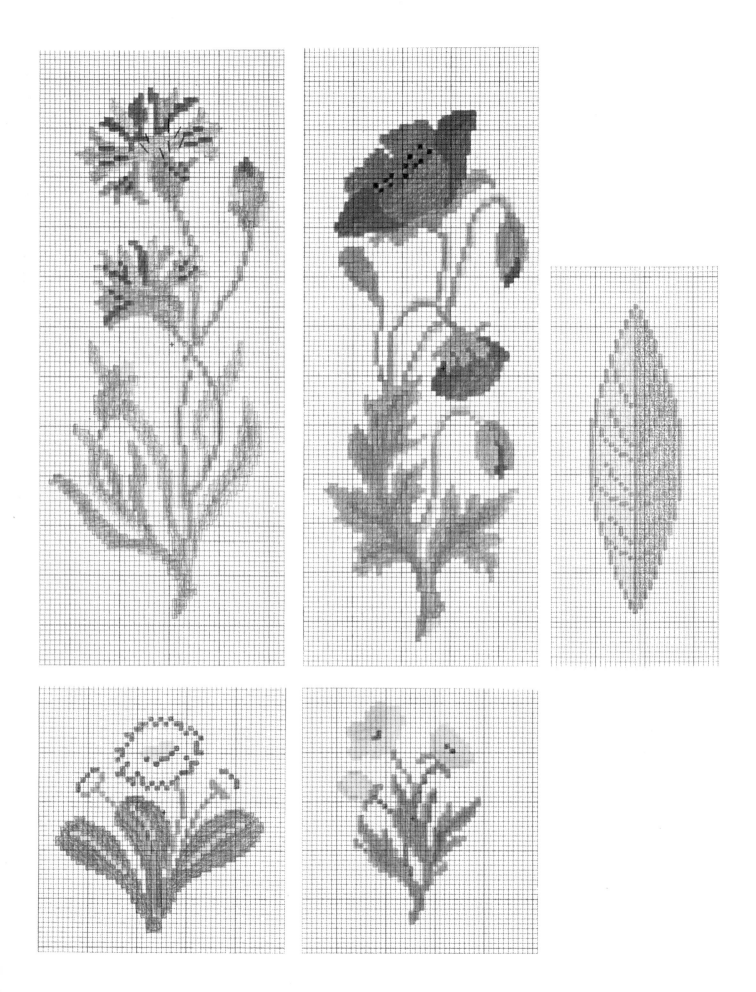

FLOWER TILES

I have long coveted William De Morgan's tiles. As a friend and colleague of William Morris, they worked together on many designs. De Morgan combined the techniques of lustre decoration with the artistry of the Pre-Raphaelite period to create a wealth of ceramics – dishes, vases, tiles – many of which are now valuable assets in private and public collections throughout the world.

De Morgan's fabulous creations caused me problems, though, because the bright glaze colours do not reproduce well in wool. I have contented myself therefore with his excellent draughtsmanship and have tried to match the colours as closely as possible from Appleton's wide range.

Many years ago, I started work on a needlepoint version of one of De Morgan's exotic peacocks, but the wonderful simplicity of needlepoint 'tiles' came some time later. The charming single *Rose* and his stylized interpretation of *Carnation* can be seen at the Victoria and Albert Museum in London. As needlepoint projects, they have many advantages. They are the easiest in the book, and they can be stitched in the shortest time with the minimum amount of concentration. They are small and thus portable – perfect for a long journey, a holiday or as an introduction to needlepoint. They can be made into scatter cushions, or sewn together with other 'tiles' to form a rug – the idea being that you do not need to carry around (or invest in) the complete materials for a rug at the outset, but can work on it in small, manageable sections. The pink and blue colourways with dark blue and light grey backgrounds give the classic effect of De Morgan's own work.

These tile designs also look charming in miniature, worked on fine canvas, as covers or cushions for dolls' furniture or as pincushions.

The *Carnation* tile has a more overall design – again, I used two of the original colour schemes and the

Above: A *Carnation* cushion made by stitching four tiles together on finer 12 to the inch canvas (see page 95).

Left: Rose tiles made up into a cushion and rug, in the Green Room at Kelmscott Manor. The tiles at the base of the fireplace are Morris and Co's artichoke design of 1870. The chair is by Rossetti.

cream background. The choice of brown as an alternative is my own invention. The complementary colours could also be combined to make an attractive rug.

The *Carnation* cushion is worked on a finer canvas and shows the design closer in size to De Morgan's original tiles. It is worked from the same charts, but with the flowers tilted four ways.

The *Chrysanthemum* series of tiles from which my rug design evolved is quite luscious. It features full, fat flowers and curling leaves – how beautiful they must have looked in a bathroom! Sadly, the very bright turquoise fronds looked garish in wool so I had to leave them out; I also replaced the turquoise buds with lavender and pink ones. I had to end the leaves naturally so that they did not run off the edge, and I added a border. The leaves could not be shaded on the coarser canvas so they were simplified. Despite all this, the colours and the feeling are as close as I could make them to De Morgan's, though I do have a sneaking desire to see the flowers on a dark background!

Right: Red walls provide a dramatic background to the *Carnation* cushion and rug.

Below: Chrysanthemum rug and *Rose* cushions shown in a romantic setting at the Red House. The antique croquet set was used by William Morris and his friends.

INSTRUCTIONS – Rose Tile

Size

Design area: 77 × 74 stitches

Size of the finished design: 10^1/$_2$ × 10 in (27 × 25.5 cm)

Size of the finished tile: (cushion) 12 × 12 in (30.5 × 30.5 cm), (rug) 13 × 13 in (33 × 33 cm)

Materials

8-mesh single canvas, 4 in (10 cm) larger each way than required area

Size 16 tapestry needle

Appleton's tapestry wool:

Pink rose

☐	A	pale pink (221) – 4 skeins
▨	B	mid pink (222) – 1 skein
▦	C	dark pink (223) – 1 skein
☐	D	pale green (352) – 4 skeins
▨	E	mid green (402) – 4 skeins
▨	F	dark green (405) – 1 skein
■	G	terracotta (128) – 1 skein

Background: *either* pastel (875) *or* very dark blue (929) – 2 hanks, 4 skeins

Blue rose

A	pale blue (561) – 4 skeins
B	mid blue (563) – 1 skein
C	dark blue (565) – 1 skein
D	pale green (352) – 4 skeins
E	mid green (402) – 4 skeins
F	dark green (405) – 1 skein
G	charcoal (998) – 1 skein

Background: *either* pastel (875) *or* very dark blue (929) – 2 hanks, 4 skeins

Order of stitching

Check the canvas is an exact square 4 in (10 cm) larger than the intended worked area. Use a pencil and mark 2 in (5 cm) in from the edge to define the outer limit of stitching.

If you are making a rug, the selvedge must run down the side of the canvas when you work, so that the selvedges will all run the length of the rug. You may wish to alter the position of the roses. Plan this before you start, and when you work ensure that all the stitches will lie in the same direction on the finished rug.

Find the centre of the canvas and mark with bright-coloured sewing thread. This corresponds to the centre of the chart.

The whole tile is worked in cross stitch (see page 107), using one thread of wool in the needle. (Each square on the chart represents one stitch.) Stitch the flower first, before the background.

In the rug opposite and on page 88, one row of the alternative background colour was stitched on the fourth row in from the edge of each tile to make an attractive finish.

Check that the background is square in measurement, if not in stitches. If you are making a rug, work all the other squares to exactly the same size. See page 109 for making up the rug.

If you decide to stitch the rug in one piece instead of separate 'tiles', making it up will of course be much easier. Decide on the mesh of canvas and size of rug you want, taking into account the number of stitches in the design. If it is to be equivalent to six tiles, then the length will be 50% more than the width. Decide if you want a border all round the rug and make allowances for this. Trim the canvas width if you need to. Mark 2 in (5 cm) in from the raw edge,

Top right: The *Rose* tile rug and two cushions (worked in different colourways), shown in the garden at Standen.

Bottom right: A most appropriate place for De Morgan tile design, the *Rose* tile cushion is quite at home amongst this lovely collection of china at Kelmscott Manor.

then if necessary mark the border area. Divide the central panel equally into six squares. Mark the centre of each, which corresponds to the centre of the chart. Complete the designs before stitching the background.

INSTRUCTIONS – Carnation Tile

Size
Design area: 82 × 81 stitches

Size of the finished design: 11 × 11 in (28 × 28 cm)

Size of the finished tile: 12 × 12 in (30.5 × 30.5 cm)

Materials
8-mesh single canvas, 4 in (10 cm) larger each way than the size of the required worked area

Size 16 tapestry needle

Appleton's tapestry wool:

Yellow tile

☐	A	pale yellow (841) – 4 skeins
☐	B	mid yellow (471) – 4 skeins
■	C	dark yellow (694) – 4 skeins
▨	D	pale green (251) – 4 skeins
▨	E	dark green (244) – 4 skeins
▨	F	mid green (242) – 1 hank

Background: dark brown (585) – 2 hanks

Red and yellow tile

▨	G	dark yellow (694) – 4 skeins
■	H	red (207) – 4 skeins
☐	I	mid yellow (471) – 4 skeins
▨	J	pale green (251) – 4 skeins
▨	K	dark green (244) – 4 skeins
▨	L	mid green (242) – 1 hank

Background: ivory (882) – 2 hanks

Order of stitching
Check that the canvas is an exact square 4 in (10 cm) larger than the intended worked area – trim if necessary. Using a hard pencil, mark 2 in (5 cm) in from the edge of the canvas to define the outer limit of stitching.

If you are making a rug, the selvedge must run down the side of the canvas when you work, so that the selvedges will all run the length of the rug. Plan the position of the carnations before you start so that you ensure all the stitches lie in the same direction on the finished rug.

Find the centre of the canvas and mark with bright-coloured sewing thread. This corresponds to the central mark on the chart (not the mark in the corner).

The whole tile is worked in cross stitch (see page 107), using one thread of wool in the needle. (Each square on the chart represents one stitch.) Stitch the design before the background.

Check that the background is square in measurement, if not in stitches; if you are making a rug, work all the other squares to exactly the same size. See page 109 for making up the rug.

If you decide to stitch the rug in one piece instead of separate tiles, then the making up will, of course, be much easier. Decide on the mesh of canvas and size of rug you want, taking into account the number of stitches in the design. If it is to be equivalent to six tiles, then the length will be 50% longer than the width. Trim the canvas width if you need to. Mark 2 in (5 cm) in from the raw edge and divide the central panel equally into six squares. Mark the centre of each, which corresponds to the mark in the centre of the chart. Stitch the designs before the background, remembering that each pair has one design facing in a different direction – use the photograph on page 91 as a guide.

See page 109 for finishing this rug.

Above: Carnation tile rug and cushion in front of a hand-painted door at the Red House, Bexleyheath. On the wall are panels of Morris's *Trellis* and *Daisy* designs.

INSTRUCTIONS – Carnation Cushion

Size
Design area: 163 × 163 stitches
Size of the finished design: $14^1/_2 \times 14^1/_2$ in
(37 × 37 cm)
Size of the finished cushion:
$14^1/_2 \times 14^1/_2$ in (37 × 37 cm)

Materials
12-mesh single canvas, 4 in (10 cm)
larger each way than the size of the
required worked area, including the
background

Size 18 or 20 tapestry needle

Appleton's tapestry wool:

    A pale yellow (841) – 4 skeins

    B mid yellow (471) – 4 skeins

    C dark yellow (694) – 4 skeins

    D pale green (251) – 1 hank

    E mid green (242) – 1 hank

    F dark green (244) – 4 skeins

    H red (866) or (207)) – 4 skeins

Background: dark brown (585) – 4
hanks, sufficient to extend the background one row beyond the design

Order of stitching
The entire design can be worked in tent
stitch (see page 106), using one thread of
wool in the needle.

    Fold the canvas in half each way to
find the centre. Baste along the fold lines
with bright-coloured sewing thread.

    The centre of the finished design is in
the corner of both charts. (Each square
represents one stitch.) Count from the
centre to the curved mid green base of
one of the quarters, then complete the
rest of the design as on page 89. The
charts need to be turned upside down to
register the centre point each time –
make sure they are equidistant apart.

INSTRUCTIONS – Chrysanthemum Rug

Size
Design area: 259 stitches long × 183 stitches wide
Size of the finished rug, including border: 30 × 43 in (76.5 cm × 1m 10 cm)

Materials
6-mesh canvas, 4 in (10 cm) larger each way than the required worked area

Size 16 tapestry needle

Appleton's tapestry wool:

- light green (352) – 12 hanks

- mid green (355) – 3 hanks, 4 skeins

- darkest green (294) – 2 hanks, 4 skeins

- pale pink (141) – 2 hanks

- mid pink (142) – 2 hanks

- darkest pink (143) – 1 hank, 4 skeins

- pale blue (741) – 2 hanks

- mid blue (743) – 2 hanks

- darkest blue (746) – 1 hank, 4 skeins

Background: ivory (882) – 13 hanks

Order of stitching
The entire rug is worked in cross stitch (see page 107). Use two threads of wool in the needle throughout.

Fold the canvas in half both ways to find the centre. Baste along the fold lines with bright-coloured sewing thread. If you prefer to work with a frame, see pages 102–3.

Find the centre mark on the chart. Each square on the chart represents one stitch. Count from the centre to the pink bud and stitch this first.

When half the design is complete, turn the chart upside down and stitch the second half. The central buds are stitched in different colours – one pink and one blue.

Complete the design before stitching the border and the background.

See page 109 for suggestions on how to complete and back your rug.

Below: The *Chrysanthemum* rug, showing the entire design.

NEEDLEPOINT BASICS

William Morris advocated 'art made by the people and for the people as a joy both to the maker and the user'. Once you have become involved in the creativity of needlepoint and completed your first piece of work, you will want to repeat the process again and again.

The designs in this book vary in their complexity only by the quantity of colours and the size and mesh of the canvas. The same basic rules apply to all of them. I would hesitate to recommend a beginner to start with *Acanthus* (page 68), but with a little practice on small projects all the designs are undoubtedly well within your scope.

Before beginning the embroidery, there are some basic decisions to be made. Which design do you prefer? What use will it be put to? Where will be its likely place in the home? Once these points are settled, you can then choose the most suitable canvas and threads.

All the designs are stitched on single (mono) canvas or interlocked rug canvas. The thread quantities quoted are for the size and mesh of the canvas used for the pieces of work illustrated in the photographs. It might be simpler, for your first project, to stay with the same format. If you want to change the colours to suit a particular room setting, this is

easy to do if you take a little care. The *Magpies* design (page 61) is a good example. Sometimes a change of background colour is sufficient, as in *Wild Flowers* (page 44) and *Lodden* (page 30). If you are not sure how the colours will look together, work a sample of the design first.

How to start

Whatever you decide to make, you need to mark out the background area. If you are making a fitted design, such as a chair seat, see page 104.

Start in the centre of the canvas. Fold the canvas in half each way, then mark the folds by basting along them with bright-coloured sewing thread. This divides the design into quarters which makes it easier for you to count from the chart.

If you decide to use a frame, now is the time to fix the canvas to it. Otherwise, you may want to overstitch or bind the edges of the canvas to prevent them fraying and catching your clothes.

Identify all your threads – it may help to label each shade with the corresponding Appleton's wool code from the chart. You do not have to use wool (see 'Threads', page 100). The colours quoted in the key to each chart apply to that chart only. If you have some yarn left over and wish to use it for another project, check you have the right colours by referring to the Appleton's code numbers rather than the names.

Find the centre of the chart and thread your needle with the colour nearest to that point. Use the specified number of threads in the needle, to ensure good coverage of the canvas, and knot the end. You are now ready to start stitching.

Take the thread down from above the canvas at a point which will soon be covered by the same, or similar, colour about 1½ in (3 cm) away from the starting point. The thread will be worked over at the back and secured. Cut off the knot when you reach it with your stitching. Finish off either by threading through a line of stitches at the back, or

by bringing the thread up 1½ in (3 cm) away from the last stitch and working over it before cutting off the loose end.

Stitch the design before the background. Each square on the chart (not intersection) represents 1 stitch (across an intersection) on the canvas. When the needlepoint is complete, see page 108.

It really is as simple as it sounds, but for those who wish to experiment or who feel secure knowing a little more, here are some technical details.

Choosing the canvas

Canvas is made in a range of materials, including cotton, linen, man-made fibres and plastic. The best-quality canvas readily available is made from polished cotton. A needlepoint embroidery should, with care, last several lifetimes so it makes sense to buy the best you can afford.

There are three main types of canvas: single (or mono), interlocked and double thread (Penelope). All are meant to have an even weave of open-mesh squares. However, you can sometimes detect a slight difference in the length and width; if you ever need to join two pieces, be careful that the selvedges lie in the same direction.

Single canvas consists of a weave of single threads, and is graded according to the number of threads per inch. It is ideal for the tent stitch that is used for most of the designs in this book. Interlocked canvas has the threads twisted so that they 'lock' at the intersections. Double-thread canvas has pairs of threads running each way, and is graded according to the number of holes per inch. Needlepoint stitches are normally worked over pairs of threads.

The choice of canvas is very much a matter of personal taste, but my preference is for good-quality single canvas. With the exception of firm rug canvases, interlocked canvas is often far too thin for hard wear. The interlocking is intended to prevent the canvas threads shifting with the tension of the stitches, but unless the work is firmly framed the canvas is so thin and pliable that it will

Left: What lovely things to work with – an antique *chatelaine* and other needlework tools, shown with my adaptation of Morris's *Medway* wallpaper as an embroidery.

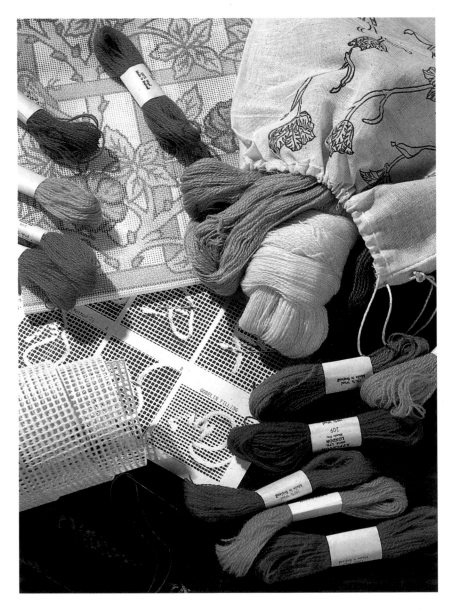

pairs and stitching over one thread only. This is generally done when intricate details are required, for example, to stitch the features of a face. Sometimes the entire design area may be worked this way, in *petit point*, leaving the background to be worked over pairs of threads in *gros point*.

The second advantage of double canvas is that it may be trammed. When needlepoint embroidery is trammed, long stitches are run across the canvas, to be covered later by tent stitches in the same colour. The whole design is trammed before the real stitching begins, and decisions about where colours should lie are taken at this early stage. Devotees of tramming believe that it increases the wear of the article by leaving a double thickness of thread on the surface. One could, however, argue that the topstitching will wear as soon and need repair just like an untrammed canvas.

When buying canvas, always allow for at least 2 in (5 cm) of spare canvas all round the required finished size of the embroidery for stretching or blocking.

Changing the size of the design

If you want to enlarge or reduce the design, you will need a different mesh canvas. Simply divide the number of stitches in the design (quoted on each pattern page) by the size required (not including the background). The answer will be the canvas mesh you need. Check both the width and height of the design.

For example, if you want a design 12 in (30 cm) wide and the number of the stitches on the chart is 144, you will need 12-mesh canvas. If the division does not produce a round number, choose a finer mesh and make up the extra size in the background colour.

Threads

I have used my favourite Appleton's wools because of their fabulous range of colours. Each shade is produced in both crewel and tapestry wool.

Crewel is a fine, twisted, 2-ply yarn

Above: The contents of one of my Designer's Forum kits, which contain all you need to make up your chosen design.

tend to pull out of shape. It is then extremely difficult to stretch it back, as it will not take any great degree of tension without breaking. My advice is never to use it for chair seats or anything large, and always use a frame. Rug canvas is the exception to this rule; all the rugs in this book are designed to be embroidered in cross stitch on a strong, interlocked rug canvas with either six or eight holes to the inch.

Double canvas has two advantages over the others. As the threads run in pairs in each direction, a 12-mesh canvas, which would normally be worked with the stitches crossing pairs of threads, can be transformed into a much finer 24-mesh canvas by separating the which may be used as a single thread (as in the doll's chair background) or up to five or six threads in the needle for the coarsest canvas. Threading several strands into the needle may sound a nuisance, but you will find it is quite simple to do. The advantages are that the wool lies very flat when worked, and you have the opportunity to experiment with blending the shades in the needle. If the shades are close, you will create a new colour (as in the background of *Acanthus*, page 68). If they are quite contrasting, then you will have an interesting tweedy effect. The mixing of colours works well in *Tiffany Window* (page 41), where the clouds blend gently into the sky with no harsh edges.

Tapestry wool is thicker than crewel wool, the equivalent of 4-ply yarn. There is no reason why you should not use it in any of the designs in this book if they are on a 14-mesh or coarser mesh canvas, and if you do not need to blend shades in the needle. I have used it for the rugs: a single thread for the finer rug canvas and two threads for the coarser canvas, in both cases using cross stitch which covers the canvas more efficiently.

Although my preference is for Appleton's wools because of the excellent range of colours, you may be accustomed to another brand. Take a little time to choose complementary colours.

There are also many types of cotton and silk threads – stranded and twisted, with shiny and matt finishes. These threads will not wear as well as wool and are generally more suited to finer work – the design on the doll's chair was worked in a mixture of the two. They are more expensive than wool but provide an even greater range of colours and textures to play with. Either can be used with wool to great effect – the sheen provided by a group, or line, of silk stitches next to wool brings to life the light on a wet leaf; black silk would give the eyes of the *Magpies* a gleam; and the feathers on the birds in *Tiffany Window* can be made to shine in the sunlight. Experiment with other threads, you will find it most rewarding.

To calculate quantities of wool, the general rule is that one hank of wool, which weighs 25 grams (just under 1 oz), will cover an area 6 × 6 in (15 × 15 cm) in tent stitch. This has to be approximate, and it does assume that you are using enough wool in the needle to cover the canvas and not so much that it is difficult to pull through.

If you need to be very precise in your estimates, you can stitch a sample square and note exactly how much wool is used: allow more than the eventual calculation as you have to take into account the irregularities of shapes around the design. Generally, longer stitches use less wool even though an extra strand of crewel wool would be needed.

It is not crucial if you under-estimate the quantities of wool for the design – if the dye has changed, you will have an extra shade to work with. The background wool is more important; even the slightest change will show when stitching and this cannot always be readily noticed simply by holding the hanks together in your hand. If you have to buy extra wool for the background, try and find the same dye lot, although dye lot numbers are not always shown on embroidery threads. Always blend some of the old thread with the new in the needle for a few rows to prevent a hard line. This is only possible with crewel wool; if you are using tapestry wool, try and stagger the line between the old and new.

Needles

The blunt-ended, large-eyed tapestry needles come in sizes 13 (for the coarsest canvas) to 26 (for very fine work). The needle needs to be easily threaded with the required thickness of wool and to be able to pass through the canvas without tugging. Appropriate needle sizes are given for each of the designs in the book and are generally 22 for 18- or 17-mesh canvas, 20 for 14- or 13-mesh canvas, 18 for 12- or 10-mesh, and 16 for 8- or 6-mesh canvas. When I work, I like to have several needles, each threaded with a different colour.

Frames

Not everyone enjoys using a frame, but they do have several advantages. By keeping the canvas evenly stretched, a frame minimizes the distorting effect of diagonal stitches. Both hands are free so that one hand may be used above and one below the canvas, passing the needle through from one to the other, which speeds up the stitching process. The stitches are also more even than those made with the single 'scooping' movement used when the canvas is hand-held.

The golden rule is that each embroiderer should enjoy the work, so decide which type of frame, if any, is most suitable for you. There are three main types of frame to choose from:

Slate frame Slate frames are used by professional embroiderers. They can be rested on trestles, against a table or attached to a floor stand.

This is a strong frame, heavier than other frames, and enables the canvas to be pulled very taut. It consists of two roller bars with webbing, and two side pieces that slot into the rollers at top and bottom. These are held in place either with split pins or wooden screws. The rather time-consuming process of framing up is rewarded by the ease of stitching.

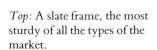

Top: A slate frame, the most sturdy of all the types of the market.

Right: Two sizes of travel frame – *above* (with a new De Morgan tile design in the making), an 18-inch frame, and *below*, a 12-inch type.

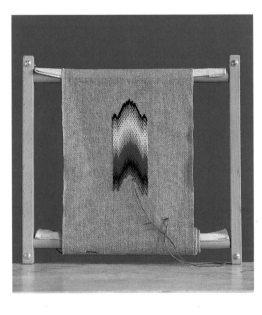

Square travel frame This is a lighter, less substantial version of the slate frame, with shorter side bars, exposing less of the canvas. The side bars are attached to the roller bar with wing nuts, so an even tension cannot be achieved as the nuts tend to slip. This frame, however, is easy to dismantle and transport.

The size of the frame you will need is determined by the width of the canvas. The webbing on the frame, which denotes its size, must not be smaller than the canvas width. The length of the canvas is less important as the excess can be rolled round the bars after being attached, and worked in sections.

Ring or hoop frame More often used for surface embroidery, this kind of frame can also be suitable for smaller pieces of canvaswork. The canvas is stretched over the inner ring, the outer ring holding it firmly in place. A hoop can be used with a table or floor stand, but the work must be removed from the frame after every session. Unless the piece is very small, you will need to move the ring from area to area as you work. Clearly, the work is portable, with or without the hoop.

Some embroiderers believe that the hoop marks the work, but I have found that any creases are removed in the stretching process.

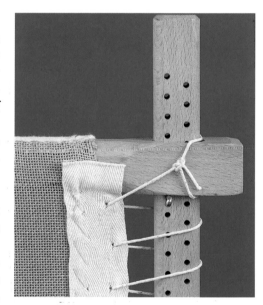

How to frame on a slate frame
You will need webbing, button thread and string. Mark the centre of the canvas by folding the canvas in half each way and basting along the folds with bright-coloured sewing thread. Sew a strip of webbing to each side of the canvas, using button thread and straight stitches 1 in (2.5 cm) in from the edge of the canvas, as shown. (You can, if you prefer, machine stitch this.)

Fold the canvas under ¹/₂ in (1 cm) at top and bottom. Match the centre to the centre of the webbing on the frame bars. Pin from the centre outwards and oversew. At all times, use the threads of the canvas to ensure that everything is exactly square.

Insert the slats into the ends of the frame bars and position the pegs an equal number of holes from the top. Repeat at the bottom, pulling as tightly as possible. If the canvas is too long, you may need to roll it round the tape bars, leaving the centre exposed. When the exposed part is complete, you will need to unstring and re-roll the canvas, and then re-string.

To string the canvas, use a large-eyed needle (a packing needle is ideal). Lace the string between the side bars and the side webbing, pull it up as tightly as possible and knot the string securely. The canvas must be absolutely square and taut.

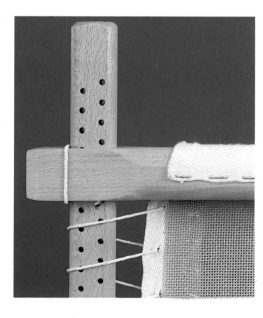

Top: A ring frame, with the *Rose* tile (see page 92) partially made.

Centre and below: Front (top) and back (below) view of the framed canvas.

Making a template

For special shapes, such as a chair seat, you will need a template, an exact replica of the shape you wish to cover. An upholsterer can supply you with one, or you can make one yourself with a square of old sheeting or muslin. This will indicate the complete area to be stitched. If the chair has lost its stuffing, pad it out to its anticipated shape before starting.

Fold the template fabric in half in both directions to find the centre and mark the centre lines – horizontally and verti-cally. Lay it squarely on the seat and hold in place along the centre (measur-ing first to find the centre of the seat). Smooth the template down and mark carefully round the line of the outside area, where there may already be a line of upholsterer's tacks – this should be to the outer extremities of the tacked area, leaving the unworked canvas for tuck-ing in.

If the chair has a long drop at the front, it is possible that the centre of the template will not fall in the centre of the seat (i.e. where the centre of the design should also be). Mark the ideal design centre onto the template. Trim round the outline. Your canvas should be at least 2 in (5 cm) larger all round. Tidy the outline of the template either on the fabric or by transferring it to paper. Check that the shape is symmetrical.

Lay the template on the canvas and mark the centre point to coincide with the centre point of the template, ensur-ing that the horizontal and vertical lines of the template lie squarely along the threads of the canvas. Mark the canvas round the edges of the template, using indelible ink. Keep the template so that you can check it against your work later if necessary.

Charts

Although they may appear daunting to the uninitiated, charts offer several advantages over printed canvases.

It is great fun to start with a plain can-vas and watch the design grow as you stitch. With a printed canvas, there is less scope for large errors and you add to the colour and texture as you work, but the element of surprise is lacking.

There are moments in the stitching of printed canvases where, for instance, the edge of a petal lies between two canvas threads. A decision must be made as to which thread to cover with your stitches, perhaps making the petal sig-nificantly larger or smaller. In charts there is no such ambiguity.

The most obvious advantage of charts is their adaptability (page 105).

How to work from a chart

The basic rules have already been given on page 99. You can mark the centre lines with an indelible pen, but if this is too dark and the thread colour is light you will run the risk of it showing through. If pencil is used, it should be hard as it tends to rub off on the threads, making them dirty.

Identifying and marking the threads is helpful if you are likely to be working in different lights. Shades that are close may be difficult to distinguish at night.

With a printed canvas, the overlying parts of the design are always worked first. This ensures that where there may be some doubt as to where exactly to place the stitches, the topmost shapes are given priority and a good line. The chart takes away any doubt, so you may stitch in any order you wish. I like to have sev-eral needles threaded so that I can pro-gress out from the centre, working on different colours as I come to them without re-threading the needle.

For a symmetrical design, you may find it helpful to stitch the matching sec-tion on the other half immediately you have finished the first. Here, again, threaded needles are time-saving.

It is much safer to stitch the design first. If you do miscount and feel you want to unpick, it is very distressing to have to unpick the background too!

In this book, only half of some of the charts for symmetrical designs is shown. When you are working the second half of the design, you can use a mirror propped at right angles against

the chart to help you 'see' the other side. I find that following the photograph helps prevent me losing my sense of direction. Where only a quarter of the design is shown as a chart, this is repeated (with the chart turned upside down) in the diagonally opposed quarter. The other two quarters are mirror images of the first two.

Adapting charts

This is the joy of charts. If you want to increase or decrease the size of the design to fit a specific space, this can be done by omitting part of the design, by repeating some parts, or, more simply, by changing the mesh of the canvas (see page 100).

My doll's chair (above) shows how *Lodden I* was adapted. The canvas mesh is 28 threads to 1 in (2.5 cm), an 'antique' piece, to achieve the finished size of 5 × 5 in (13 × 13 cm). The outer foliage was left out, the two tiny open flowers were moved inwards by nine stitches and joined directly to the bud above, and the two leaves were worked on opposite corners so that they curved inwards. This has transformed a rectangular design into a square one without losing any of its charm – and also reduced it to less than half its size.

Spring Flowers (page 85) can be elongated by adding the smaller flowers to each end of the design. They could just as easily have been omitted from the original to make a much narrower design consisting of daffodils and irises only. You could also repeat more of these larger flowers to create a wider piece of embroidery.

Occasionally, just one section of a design is all you need. A particularly appealing example of this use of charts is to be found at Kelmscott Manor, in Gloucestershire, where the birds from *Strawberry Thief II* and *III* have been used to decorate the kneelers in the church where William Morris and his family are buried. This was the charming idea of Jean Wells who, with Richard Dufty, has done so much to maintain and enhance Kelmscott Manor on behalf of the Society of Antiquaries.

Left: A detail of *Lodden I* – see how the original design is adapted to fit the much smaller square of this doll's chair. The design is worked in silks and cottons, and the background in wool. The canvas is antique, and 28-to-the-inch.

105

Stitches

Where threads provide colour, stitches give texture to your work. Using a different stitch for the background will emphasize the outline of the design.

Although there are hundreds of needlepoint stitches for you to try, the ones that I have used for the designs in this book are shown on these pages.

My instructions may seem rather pre-cise, but they are meant to help you to achieve the results you see in the photographs. But rules, as we all know, are made to be broken, and with some good evenweave canvas and a needleful of thread what can be more enjoyable than experimenting? You may rediscover some old stitches or invent some new ones. As I am sure I have said before, enjoy yourself – this is *your* creation.

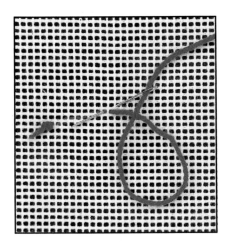

Tent stitch (Continental) This is the most frequently used of all needlepoint stitches. It is ideal for describing fine detail and creates a hard-wearing fabric that is excellent for upholstery. The long stitches on the reverse side of the canvas help to cushion and protect the work.

Tent stitch (basketweave). *Left and below* This is used for larger areas, particularly backgrounds. The 'basket-weave' effect of the stitches on the reverse of the canvas helps to prevent the canvas from becoming distorted. Work each alternate row in the opposite direction to avoid 'ridges'.

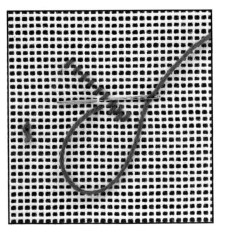

Cross stitch A hard-wearing stitch ideal for rugs and larger pieces, cross stitch also helps to eliminate distortion of the canvas. Make sure that all the crosses are formed in the same way, with the top stitches all lying in the same direction.

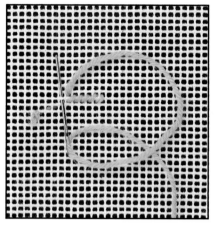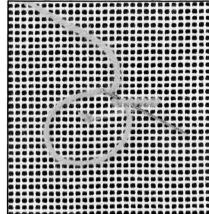

Cashmere stitch This is a useful stitch for creating a textured effect over large areas of background. It is harder-wearing than gobelin filling, but not as durable as tent stitch.

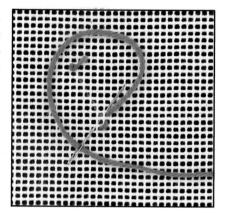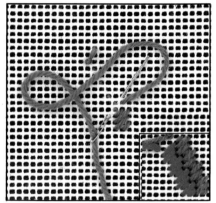

Gobelin filling A useful stitch for covering background areas quickly and creating an attractive textured effect. It is not as hard-wearing as tent stitch, so is not recommended for chair seats.

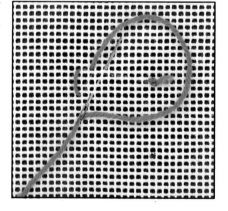

Brick stitch Similar in appearance to gobelin filling, this is useful for backgrounds. It does not wear as well as tent or cross stitch.

Note When you are working long stitches such as gobelin filling, cashmere or brick stitch, work shorter stitches where necesssary to accommodate the shapes of the design.

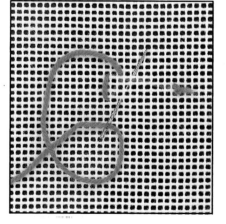

Stitching

If you will be stitching with the work held in your hand, before you begin you may prefer to hem the edges of the canvas or seal them with strips of masking tape in order to prevent them fraying or snagging on your clothes. You will find it easier to work if you roll the canvas up, leaving exposed only the area on which you are working.

How you should start and finish is explained earlier on page 99. The number of threads to be used in the needle should be sufficient to cover the canvas without being difficult to pull through the holes.

The longest thread which I would recommend is 30 in (77 cm), and this is also convenient to cut from an Appleton's hank. Longer threads may become thin by pulling through the canvas too frequently, and they may also knot and interfere with the rhythm of your work.

It is better to make stitches in two distinct movements, inserting the needle with the top hand and pushing it back up with the lower hand. This is easy if you are using a frame, but not so easy if the work is held in the hand. 'Scooping' your stitches in a single movement, although quicker, causes greater distortion of the canvas, but if you have always stitched this way you will have found that the finished work can be 'stretched' back into shape provided your tension is not too tight.

Stretching or blocking

As you stitch, even if you are using a frame, the diagonal slope of the stitches will gradually pull the canvas more and more out of true. Fortunately, both canvas and wool are pliable enough to be pulled back into shape by stretching.

To stretch a needlepoint, you will require the following: carpet tacks or fine stainless steel nails; a hammer; a large set-square (T-square); a clean cloth, larger than the canvas; and a clean board. The board must be larger than the canvas and soft enough to take tacks easily. An old clean table, or even a

wooden floor, might be suitable for a rug, but remember you will mark the wood.

Pin the cloth to the board. Dampen the back of the needlepoint and lay it face down on the cloth. Line up one edge of the needlepoint with a ruler or the edge of the board and tack it in place, placing the tacks 1 in (2.5 cm) away from the edge of the stitching and approximately $^1/_2$ in (12 mm) apart. Do not hammer them home as they will almost certainly need to be moved.

Pull the canvas and tack down an adjacent edge, using the set-square to check that the corner is a right angle. Continue round the edge, re-damping the work and pulling it, replacing tacks as necessary. When you have finished, the worked piece should be taut, with right-angled corners. This process is hard on the hands and takes a good deal of strength. The final tacks may need to be fixed at $^1/_4$ in (6 mm) intervals. If you have used a template, it will fit perfectly if the canvas is stretched correctly.

Allow the canvas to dry out slowly, leaving it for at least 36 hours before you remove the tacks. If the piece has been very badly pulled out of shape, you may need to repeat the process several times.

Mounting for framing

If you intend to frame your finished needlepoint like *Daffodils* (left), it must first be backed. You will need a piece of heavy card, calico, thread, pins and glue.

After stretching the embroidery, measure and cut the card to the exact finished worked size. Cut the calico approximately 5 in (13 cm) larger each way than the card. Place the card over the calico; cut across the corners of the calico at an angle, and bring the edges to the back of the card. Glue the calico to the board, putting glue along the raw edge of the fabric only. Allow the glue to dry.

Trim the canvas to leave an unworked border of approximately 1 in (2.5 cm) all round, and cut diagonally across at the corners. Lay the covered

Above: Daffodils (see page 59), framed in pickled pine.

side of the board on the wrong side of the needlepoint. Bring the edges of the canvas up over the board, and hold them in place by pinning through the edge of the unworked border into the thickness of the board.

Make sure that the needlepoint is correctly positioned and is held firmly, then herringbone stitch the unworked canvas border to the calico at the back of the board. Stitch just inside the glued edge of the calico and mitre the corners. Remove the pins and back with a piece of cotton or suitable fabric, slip stitching all round.

Lining and backing rugs

Stretching or blocking will improve the look of a rug, even if it has not lost its shape during stitching. If you cannot do this, it will benefit from pressing on the wrong side with a damp cloth. If the rug is out of shape, it must be stretched, either at home or professionally.

The type of backing you choose will depend in part on the use to which you intend to put the rug. A floor rug will require a more substantial backing than a rug that is to be used as a wall hanging or a sofa throw.

After stretching, trim the unworked canvas to between 2–3 in (5–7.5 cm) all round.

Fold the unworked canvas to the back and herringbone stitch it to the reverse side of the rug, using strong cotton thread; mitre the corners. Cut the lining to the finished worked size of the rug, plus a seam allowance of approximately 1 in (2.5 cm) all round.

Stab stitch along a central line from top to bottom and from side to side. Take a small stitch through the lining and rug and bring the needle back up, running the thread under the lining to make the next stitch. It may be advisable to make further rows of stab stitching at either side of the central line, to prevent sagging. Turn under the seam allowance of the lining and slip stitch it to the rug at the edges.

If the rug might need to take hard wear, it should be interlined with a firm curtain interlining felt, or even a carpet underfelt. Cut the interlining to the same size as the finished embroidery (seam allowances are not needed) and attach it as described above for the lining. Holland, Union cloth or a similar fabric can then be used for a final backing. Make sure that both the interlining and the backing are neatly and firmly stitched to the rug at the edges.

Making up a tiled rug

It is essential to ensure that the individual tile canvases are absolutely square – they may need stretching or at least careful ironing on the wrong side. Check with a set square.

Join the squares so that the selvedge sides all run down the length of the rug. Each adjoining side must have the same number of stitches so that the squares can be joined stitch for stitch.

Join the tiles by back stitching with double button thread. When complete, tidy up the back of the rug by herringbone stitching the loose edge of the canvas so that it lies flat. Mitre the corners. Finish the rug as described above.

Fringing rugs

Add a fringe to the rug after the edges of the canvas have been turned back and stitched to the reverse side, and before the rug has been backed. You will need a crochet hook and fringing twine or wool.

To cut the fringing into equal lengths, wind it round a firm strip of card or wooden slat of the correct width, then cut along one edge. To make a fringe 3 in (7.5 cm) deep, for example, you will need a 3 in (7.5 cm) wide strip of card, which will produce 6 in (15 cm) lengths of fringing. Fold each length of yarn in half and hook the folded loop through a hole at the edge of the finished rug. Thread the two ends through the loop and pull them tight. Repeat along the edge of the rug.

You can have fun knotting the fringe in different ways.

Above: An example of a long fringe intended for decorative knotting.

109

INDEX

(Figures in *italics* refer to illustrations)

PLACES TO VISIT

If you would like to explore or research more into the Arts & Crafts Movement, here is a list of some of the places in Great Britain which house original works. Some are public museums with well-publicized opening times; some are collections in the care of official bodies such as the National Trust or the Society of Antiquaries which are only open on specific dates; others are private homes. With the exception of the museums and galleries, you will need to write for an appointment to visit – a little patience will be well rewarded.

KELMSCOTT MANOR, Kelmscott, Lechlade, Gloucestershire (WM; DeM)
STANDEN, East Grinstead, West Sussex (WM)
RED HOUSE, Bexleyheath, Kent (WM)
WILLIAM MORRIS GALLERY, Walthamstow, London E17 (WM; DeM; B)

VICTORIA & ALBERT MUSEUM, Kensington, London SW7 (WM; DeM)
LEIGHTON HOUSE, Kensington, London W14 (DeM)
8 ADDISON ROAD, Kensington, London W14 (DeM)
WIGHTWICK MANOR, Wolverhampton, West Midlands (WM; DeM)
FITZWILLIAM MUSEUM, Cambridge (WM; DeM)
BRANGWYN HALL, Swansea, South Wales (B)
CARDIFF CASTLE, Cardiff, South Wales (DeM)
JACKFIELD TILE MUSEUM, Ironbridge Gorge, Telford, Shropshire

WM = William Morris
DeM = William De Morgan
B = Frank Brangwyn

NOTES FOR AMERICAN READERS

If you have difficulty in obtaining Appleton's wool, those manufactured by Paterna make acceptable substitutes. The following list shows the Paterna yarn code numbers equivalent to those Appleton's wools specified in this book.

Appleton	Paterna	Appleton	Paterna	Appleton	Paterna
101	313	202	406	304	401
104	312	204	485	324	512
121	474	205	872	331	644
122	473	206	871	333	643
124	484	207	870	335	D511
126	481	209	D211	342	643
128	920	221	490	351	605
141	924	222	933	352	605
142	923	223	D275	354	603
143	922	227	900	355	603
151	203	241	D531	356	601
155	533	242	652		
155	533	244	641		
156	532	251	653		
		251A	695		
		253	693		
		255	651		
		256	650		
		293	603		
		294	601		
		296	600		

Appleton	Paterna	Appleton	Paterna	Appleton	Paterna
401	613	504	950	602	324
402	612	521	525	641	523
403	611	522	523	642	D546
405	610	542	653	643	602
406	690	543	693	644	D522
444	821	544	692	645	662
448	841	545	691	691	444
456	300	547	691	692	754
462	544	551	773	694	733
463	543	552	713	695	732
464	542	553	772	697	740
471	727	561	505		
473	732	562	555		
474	725	563	555		
488	580	564	584		
		565	583		
		585	421		
		588	420		

Appleton	Paterna	Appleton	Paterna	Appleton	Paterna
703	494	841	704	901	443
706	492	842	734	926	511
708	490	861	855	929	510
741	564	863	862	965	201
743	561	866	850	972	203
746	560	871	716	973	202
751	946	872	715	974	462
754	913	873	615	976	451
755	D275	874	624	983	453
761	444	875	236	984	454
762	443	877	948	991	261
763	434	881	262	991B	260
764	413	882	263	993	220
766	D419	884	314	998	256
		886	564		

ACKNOWLEDGMENTS

Throughout my needlepoint years, my energy and enthusiasm have been sustained and encouraged by many people. I should like to thank them here.

Top of the list, naturally, are my husband Peter and my two sons Nick and Paul, who have all helped (and hindered!) in the way that only families can. Phyllis and Robert Steed have been conscientious and creative contributors for several years; I owe a lot to them. Jean Cook, Angela Khan and Selina Winter, all colleagues from my days at the Royal School of Needlework, have perfected my sketchy ideas into exquisite examples of needlework. Jack Crease and all my friends at Appleton's deserve special praise for their patience and a style and standard of service that, unhappily, has long disappeared from many industries. Linda Parry at the Victoria and Albert Museum has proved an invaluable inspiration; Ron Worrall and Barrie Smith have always been encouraging and helpful, especially with the loan of their furniture.

The beautiful photographs in this book – thank you, John Greenwood – were shot in some superb locations. My gratitude, therefore, to Mrs Jean Wells and Dr Richard Dufty, CBE at Kelmscott Manor, Mrs Jane Grundy at Standen and Mr & Mrs Edward Hollamby at Red House for allowing John and I to disrupt their lives with cameras and lights.

Thank you, also, to Maggie Pearlstine whose belief in my ability and determination to complete this project have moved mountains.

And, 'without whom none of this would have been possible', my most grateful and sincere acknowledgement is dedicated to the memory of William Morris himself. His influence will last for ever!

WHERE TO BUY COMPLETE KITS AND APPLETON'S WOOLS

All the designs in this book are available in kit form by mail order direct from Designers Forum. You have the choice of working on a beautiful and accurately hand-printed canvas or from a chart. Each kit is complete with canvas, wools, needle and clear instructions. Write to me at Designers Forum, PO Box 565, London SW1V 3PU and I will send you a brochure and price list.

For details of where Designers Forum kits may be purchased overseas, please contact:
Australia: Altamira, 34 Murphy Street, South Yarra, Victoria 3141
Far East: Heirloom Needlecrafts, 14 Woollerton Drive, Singapore 1025
USA: Potpourri Etc, PO Box 78, Redondo Beach, California 90277
New Zealand: Nancy's Embroidery Shop, 326 Tinakori Road, Thorndon, Wellington

Appleton's yarns are distributed in the USA by:
Handwork Tapestries Inc, 114B Allen Boulevard, Farmingdale NY 11735. Free toll: 1-800-645-9161. General information: 1-(516) 694-5276

Many specialist embroidery shops in the UK stock Appleton's yarns. Here is just a selection:

Berks
Crown Needlework, Shop 7, The Courtyard, 24 High Street, Hungerford.
Cheshire
Voirrey Embroidery, Brimstage Hall, Brimstage, Wirral.
Cumbria
Russells, 30 Castle Street, Carlisle.
Devon
Harberton Art W/Shop, 27 High Street, Totnes.
Dorset
Sherborne Tap. Centre, 1 Cheap Street, Sherborne.
Essex
Needlework, Bucklers Farm, Coggeshall, Nr. Colchester.
A. J. Franklin & Sons, 13a/15 St. Botolphs St. Colchester.
Colorcraft, 1 Emson Close, Saffron Walden.
Glos.
Ladies Work Society, Delabere House, New Road, Moreton-in-Marsh.

Campden Needlecraft Centre, High Street, Chipping Campden.
Hants
Tapestry Centre, 42 West Street, Alresford.
Hereford
Silver Tabby, Palma Court, Brookend Street, Ross-on-Wye.
Herts
Crafts of Stortford, 3 The Dells, South Street, Bishops Stortford.
Kent
Handicraft Shop, Northgate, Canterbury.
Seale Knitwear & Craft, 97 Camden Road, Tunbridge Wells.
Middx.
Artisan, 22 High Street, Pinner.
Norfolk
Pastymes, 5 St. Nicholas St., Diss.
Handworkers Market, 18 Chapel Yard, Albert St., Holt.
Timothy's Aunt, 75 Magdalen St., Norwich.
Northants
Abingdon Handicrafts, 1140 Abingdon Avenue, Abingdon.
Oxon
Needlecraft Centre, 56 North Street, Thame.
Surrey
Needlestyle, 5, The Woolmead, Farnham, Surrey.
Sussex
Pomegranates, East Street, Petworth.
Puncheon Craft Studio, 73 High Street, Uckfield.
Wilts
Mace & Nairn, 89 Crane Street, Salisbury.
Worcs.
Metiers d'Art, Castle House, 61 The Tything, Worcester.
Yorks.
Omar, 8 Crescent Road, Harrogate.
Teazle Embroideries, 35 Boothferry Road, Hull.
Spinning Jenny, Bradley, Keighley.
Spindle Tree Embs, Greenfield, Staveley, Knaresborough.
Highthorn Emb., Highthorn, Beadlam, Nawton, York.
Scotland
The Embroidery Shop, 51 William St. Edinburgh.
Christine Riley, 53 Barclay St, Stonehaven, Kincardineshire.
London
Frances Cotton, 11 The Market, Greenwich, S.E. 10.
Harrods, Knightsbridge, London S. W. 1
John Lewis, Oxford Street, W. 1